Multimedia Web Programming

Adrian Moore

First published 2005 by
PALGRAVE MACMILLAN
Houndmills, Basingstoke, Hampshire RG21 6XS and
175 Fifth Avenue, New York, N.Y. 10010
Companies and representatives throughout the world

PALGRAVE MACMILLAN is the global academic imprint of the Palgrave
Macmillan division of St. Martin's Press, LLC and of Palgrave Macmillan Ltd.
Macmillan® is a registered trademark in the United States, United Kingdom
and other countries. Palgrave is a registered trademark in the European
Union and other countries.

ISBN-13: 978-1-4039-0457-7
ISBN-10: 1-4039-0457-X

This book is printed on paper suitable for recycling and
made from fully managed and sustained forest sources.

A catalogue record for this book is available from the British Library.

10   9   8   7   6   5   4   3   2   1
14 13 12 11 10 09 08 07 06 05

Printed in China

Contents

Preface

Multimedia Web Programming has been written to address the need for accessible but comprehensive second-level undergraduate courses in client-side web applications development technologies.

Approach

This book introduces a range of technologies for developing interactive, animated, client-side multimedia content for web pages. It is designed to be suitable for a single semester course in Multimedia, Dynamic Web Applications Development, or Web Interface Construction. The book asumes that students have completed an introductory course in software development, and that they have some (although possibly very limited) experience of creating basic web pages.

Most modern multimedia web content is developed using third party *development* packages such as Dreamweaver and Flash. In recent years, however, web standards have begun to evolve to the extent that it is now possible to specify complex animations in text format, using native web *programming* notations. It is these new programming possibilities that are the main focus of this book.

The examples presented in this book have been developed for Microsoft Internet Explorer running under Windows. While recognising that other browsers and platforms are available, the technologies presented here are supported by IE to a greater extent than by any other browser. Although cross-browser portability is an important issue in commercial web development, the decision has been made that to consider it here would be at the expense of the breadth of material achievable in a single-semester course.

Structure

The book is organised roughly as three sections, covering three levels of client-side web development, from simple static pages, through DHTML and JavaScript, to a collection of advanced notations that provide explicit support for animation and multimedia. The three-tier structure is illustrated in the following diagram:

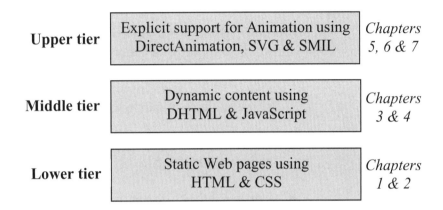

Upper tier	Explicit support for Animation using DirectAnimation, SVG & SMIL	*Chapters 5, 6 & 7*
Middle tier	Dynamic content using DHTML & JavaScript	*Chapters 3 & 4*
Lower tier	Static Web pages using HTML & CSS	*Chapters 1 & 2*

The lower tier (Chapters 1 & 2) provides the foundation for static web page construction, using HTML and Cascading Stylesheets. For students who have previous experience in web page design, this material may be treated as revision, although it is important to emphasise the separation of style information from page content.

The middle tier (Chapters 3 & 4) introduces the Document Object Model and Event Model and demonstrates how they provide a mechanism by which we can modify any style property of any element in response to some user or browser activity. We then move on to a more formal treatment of the JavaScript language, and investigate its potential for implementing programmed animations via the presentation of a simple game.

The upper tier presents three alternatives for generating animated multimedia applications without recourse to complex programming or third party applications. In Chapter 5, we introduce DirectAnimation —a set of Microsoft controls that use ActiveX objects to specify graphical and animated content. Chapter 6 presents SVG (Scalable Vector Graphics) —an XML-based notation for constructing complex vector-based graphics and animations.

Chapter 7 demonstrates how SMIL (Synchronised Multimedia Integration Language) provides a framework for the construction of interactive animated multimedia presentations, in text format.

It is important to note that this book does not aim to provide an exhaustive reference to the technologies presented. Rather, it presents a series of worked examples, which guide the reader through the subject material and encourage investigation of the online references provided at the end of each chapter.

Support

The material presented in the book is supported by a number of study aids to facilitate student learning. These include the following:

- *Chapter Objectives* highlight the main points to be studied and allow students to gauge their progress.

- *Summary* points at the end of each chapter review the main concepts introduced.

- *Further Information* at the end of each chapter provides a selection of links to relevant online resources.

- *Exercises* for each chapter provide an opportunity to extend the examples presented in the text, and to put newly acquired skills into practice.

- *Index*. A comprehensive index at the back of the book helps readers to easily locate individual concepts and examples.

- *Supporting Website*. A website for the book at http://palgrave.com/science/computing/moore/ contains working versions of all the examples in the text, links to useful resources, and a discussion forum where readers can share experiences and web development tips.

An HTML Primer

CHAPTER OBJECTIVES

In this chapter, we address the following key questions.

- What is HTML?
- What is the role of mark-up tags in HTML?
- How can we structure text within an HTML document?
- What types of list structure are available for presenting collections of related information?
- How can we manage links within and between web pages?
- How can table structures be used to manage the layout of the information on our web page?
- How do we use frames to display the contents of several pages in a single browser window?
- How can we enhance the presentation of our web page with images?
- What options are available for embedding audio and video elements within our web pages?

1.1 Introduction to HTML

HTML (Hyper Text Mark-up Language) is a notation used to describe the presentation and layout of information on web pages. The purpose of HTML contrasts with traditional programming languages, the intent of which is to describe a set of actions to be carried out in a designated order.

In HTML, the page content is *marked up* with *elements*, designated as *tags* consisting of keywords contained in pairs of angle brackets < and >. For example, the `html` element itself, which indicates that we are writing a web page to be interpreted and displayed by a browser, begins with a start tag of `<html>` and terminates with an end tag of `</html>` as shown in Figure 1.1 which illustrates a first web page.

Figure 1.1
A First Web Page

```
<!-- Figure 1.1 -->
<!-- Note the specification  of comments in HTML -->

<html>

<head>
   <title>My first web page</title>
</head>

<body>
    Welcome to my first web page.
</body>

</html>
```

2

HTML tags are not case sensitive. However it is good practice to be consistent in the way in which tags are specified. Many HTML authors prefer to use uppercase for tags to help make them stand out although lowercase is more usually preferred to ensure compatibility with the emerging XHTML standard. Also, it is important to note that white space (spaces, tabs and new lines) is insignificant in determining the layout of a web page. All consecutive white space characters in the HTML source of a document are collapsed to a single space character. If we want multiple spaces, tabs or new lines, then we must use the appropriate tags described later in this chapter.

Figure 1.1 illustrates how an HTML document is composed of **head** and **body** sections. Note the use of the `<head>`, `</head>`, `<body>` and `</body>` tags to open and close each section. The head contains various elements relating to the document as a whole — here we have given the document a **title** (using the `<title>` and `</title>` tags), but other head elements will be introduced later. The body contains the actual content to be displayed by the browser. In this document a single sentence welcomes the reader to our first web page.

1.2 Basic Text Formatting

HTML provides a number of ways for us to format the text on our web pages.

1.2.1 Line Breaks

By default, page elements are presented in a top-to-bottom, left-to-right order, and the width of the browser window determines when a new line of output is started. If we want to force the presentation of content on separate lines of output, we can use the `<br>` (line break) tag.

1.2.2 Paragraphs

Where we have a large quantity of text information, we may want to organise the text into paragraphs. The HTML paragraph tags `<p>` … `</p>` provide a container into which we place the paragraph text.

Figure 1.2 illustrates the effect of using line breaks and paragraphs to organise text on a web page.

Figure 1.2
Line Breaks and
Paragraphs

```html
<html>

<head>
  <title>Line breaks and paragraphs</title>
</head>

<body>
 <p>This is the first paragraph. All of this
    information will be displayed in a continuous flow,
    with a new line taken only when required.</p>

 <p>This is the second paragraph. Note the default space
    between paragraphs.  We will see later how to
    over-ride this default. <br> This sentence is
    presented on a new line within the same paragraph.
    Note the difference between line spacing and paragraph
    spacing.</p>
</body>

</html>
```

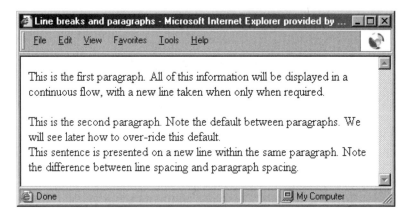

1.2.3   Headers

Headers provide a way to impose structure on our content. HTML provides 6 header types that change the size of the text based on the level (of importance) of the header. Level 1 is deemed to have the most emphasis (the largest text size) and the hierarchy proceeds down to Level 6 for the least emphasis. Figure 1.3 illustrates how to specify the 6 header styles.

Figure 1.3
Header Styles

```
<body>
  <h1>Header level 1</h1>
  <h2>Header level 2</h2>
  <h3>Header level 3</h3>
  <h4>Header level 4</h4>
  <h5>Header level 5</h5>
  <h6>Header level 6</h6>
</body>
```

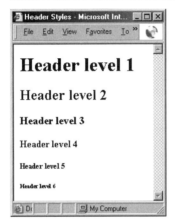

1.2.4 Special Characters

HTML makes special provision for inserting characters which are either unreachable from a standard QWERTY keyboard (such as ©, ½ and accented characters like é), or which have special meaning in HTML (such as < and >).

Such characters can be obtained by using their ASCII code e.g. `&$38;` for ASCII 38h (the ampersand character &); or by using an abbreviation of the character name e.g. `&copy;` for the copyright symbol ©; `&frac12;` for the fraction ½, and `&eacute;` for the accented character é. (Note the use of the semicolon in all cases.)

1.2.5 Advanced Text Formatting Options

HTML includes tags to implement superscript, subscript and strikethrough text, as illustrated by Figure 1.4:

Figure 1.4
Advanced Text
Formatting

```
<p><del>This line has been struck out.</del></p>

<p>The area of a circle is PI * r<sup>2</sup></p>

<p>Subscripted text can be used to indicate
   <sub>footnotes</sub>.</p>
```

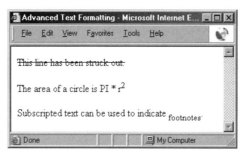

1.2.6 Other Formatting – Sizes, Colours, Styles and Alignment

From the earliest days of HTML, it has been possible to provide detailed specification of the presentation of the text on web pages. A range of HTML tags and attributes were available to achieve effects such as bold, italics or underline, while the size, colour and alignment of text, as well as the font used, could also be controlled. In latter years, however, the web development community has taken the view that the role of HTML is to represent the *content* and *structure* (the *what*?) of the information being displayed, while the details of presentation (the *how*?) should be specified separately. Hence, many of the tags and attributes that originally dealt with presentation issues have been **deprecated** (are no longer supported) by the W3C standards body although they remain understood by the vast majority of modern browsers. In this book, we adopt the W3C approach and deal with presentation issues in Chapter 2, Cascading Stylesheets.

1.2.7 Horizontal Rules

A horizontal rule is a bar of user-defined width and height, which is laid horizontally across the screen. It is a very useful device for breaking up text on a page into meaningful units to make the text easier to read. It is specified by the `<hr>` tag, which has the following attributes:

`width`	the width of the bar. The value can be specified as a percentage of the full screen width, or as an absolute size in pixels.
`size`	the height of the bar in pixels.
`align`	determines the position of the bar across the screen. `align` can be `left`, `right` or `center`. Note the United States spelling of "center"; this is a recurring theme in web development notations.
`noshade`	enables the user to eliminate the default shading and instead display the horizontal rule as a solid bar.

These attributes are illustrated by the code in Figure 1.5. Note that the horizontal rule element also inserts a line break directly below it.

Figure 1.5
Horizontal Rules

```
<hr width="50%" size="1" align="center">
<hr width="75%" size="3" align="left">
<hr width="85%" size="5" align="right">
<hr width="150" size="7" align="left" noshade>
```

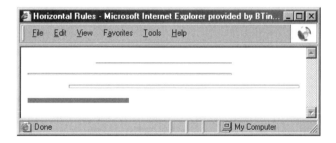

1.3   List Structures

HTML provides a number of list elements to enable us to present the information in our pages in a more structured way. Both unordered (bullet-point) and ordered (numbered/lettered) lists are available, and these are described in turn in the following sections.

1.3.1 Unordered Lists

The unordered list element creates a list where each element is preceded by a bullet mark. The list must be enclosed in `<ul>` ... `</ul>` tags, and each list element is enclosed within `<li>` ... `</li>`. Figure 1.6 illustrates the definition of a simple unordered list.

Figure 1.6
Unordered Lists

```
<p>The following programming
   languages are available
</p>

<ul>
    <li>JavaScript</li>
    <li>C++</li>
    <li>Prolog</li>
    <li>Visual Basic</li>
</ul>
```

The list item (between the `<li>` ... `</li>` tags can include any valid HTML, therefore any web presentation element can be employed to increase the visual appeal of the list.

1.3.2 Ordered Lists

An ordered list is defined by `<ol>` ... `</ol>` tags. Each item is enclosed in `<li>` ... `</li>` as before. Now, instead of the bullet, each item is numbered. By default, ordered lists use decimal sequence numbers (1, 2, 3, 4, ...), but this can be changed by including a `type` attribute in the `<ol>` tag as illustrated in Figure 1.7.

Figure 1.7
Ordered Lists

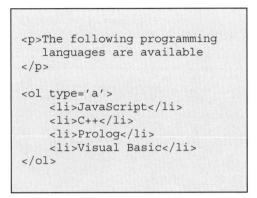

By changing the `type` attribute the style of numbering can be modified. For example, the tag `<ol type='A'>` would result in uppercase numbering in the form A, B, C, …; while `<ol type='I'>` would give uppercase Roman numbering in the form I, II, III, IV, ….

1.3.3   Definition Lists

A definition list is a useful tool for presenting information under a series of headings or subheadings, such as

> Heading 1
>   Text displayed under heading 1
>
> Heading 2
>   Text displayed under heading 2
>
> Heading 3
>   Text displayed under heading 3

This effect is achieved by the HTML code illustrated in Figure 1.8. Note the introduction of 3 new tags:

`<dl>` … `</dl>` delimits the definition list
`<dt>` … `</dt>` the definition title, or heading for the list entry
`<dd>` … `</dd>` the definition data, or content for the list entry.

Figure 1.8
Definition Lists

```
<p>The following programming languages
   are available</p>

<dl>
   <dt>JavaScript</dt>
      <dd>This is useful for adding dynamic content to Web
          pages.</dd>

   <dt>C++</dt>
      <dd>This is a object-oriented language, suitable for
          building large applications.</dd>

   <dt>Prolog</dt>
      <dd>A language best suited to the development
          of applications where the solution is described
          as a collection of rules</dd>

   <dt>Visual Basic</dt>
      <dd>A suitable tool for the development of
          event-driven interactive applications</dd>
</dl>
```

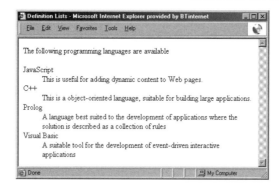

1.3.4   Nested Lists

Figure 1.9 demonstrates nested lists, where a list item is itself another list. This is useful for displaying collections of lists.

Figure 1.9
Nested Lists

```
<p>My CD Collection</p>

<ul>
    <li>The Beatles
        <ol> <li>Abbey Road</li>
             <li>Help!</li>
        </ol>
    </li>
    <li>Oasis
        <ol><li>Definitely Maybe</li>
            <li>Be Here Now</li>
        </ol>
    </li>
</ul>
```

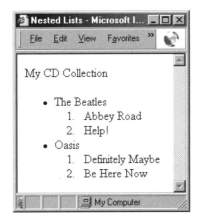

1.4   Hyperlinks

1.4.1   Linking to Other Web Pages

The World Wide Web is constructed of connected pages, where each page includes clickable links to other pages, either on the same server or elsewhere in the internet. Links are specified in HTML using anchor tags (**<a> .... </a>**). A typical anchor tag to specify a link to another page might be as follows:

<a href="nextPage.html"> click here </a>

The URL of the page at the other end of the link. A full URL can be given to refer to a page at any location on the Internet

The text that acts as the clickable link. By default, this text is underlined and coloured, but these defaults can be over-ridden.

11

1.4.2 Email Links

A hyperlink can also trigger an email message rather than a jump to another page by using the `mailto:` value for the `href` attribute. For example, the following HTML fragment will provide a link, which, whenever clicked, will open the default mail program to compose a message to the quoted address.

```
Click
<a href="mailto:a.n.other@somewhere.com">
   here </a>
to send me an email
```

1.4.3 Internal Links

Section 1.4.1 presented the concept of hyperlinks, by which we are able to specify anchors that whenever clicked cause some other page to be loaded into the browser. By default, we are positioned at the top of the new page.   Figure 1.10 illustrates *Internal Linking*, which lets us jump to *any point* within a page, including the page currently displayed in the browser. Note the position of the vertical scroll bar in each case, indicating the position within the page.

Figure 1.10
Internal Linking

```
<a name="top"></a>This is the top of the page
Jump to <a href="#middle">the middle</a>

<br><br><br>

<a name="middle"></a>This is the middle of the page
Jump to <a href="#bottom">the bottom</a>

<br><br><br>

<a name="bottom"></A>This is the bottom of the page
Jump to <a href="#top">the top</a>
```

A reference point within a page is defined by the
`<a name="here">` tag, as for **top**, **middle** and **bottom** in Figure
1.10. It is then possible to link directly to this point in the page,
either by using (e.g.) **href="#top"** if we are linking to a point on
the current page, or by using
href="http://www.somewhere.com/thisPage.html#top" if
we are linking to a point on a remote page.

1.5   Table Structures

The table is one of the most flexible and useful features of HTML.
As well as providing a way of laying out collections of raw data,
tables allow us to publish very professional looking pages by
arranging our page content into rows and columns and formatting
accordingly.

1.5.1   Basic Table Structure

A basic table consists of a **head** and a **body**, each of which may be
further subdivided into rows and columns, and a **caption**. Figure
1.11 illustrates a basic table organisation.

Figure 1.11
Basic Table Structure

```
<table border="1" width="50%">
   <caption>A Basic Table</caption>
   <thead>
      <tr>   <th>Surname</th>   <th>First Name</th>   </tr>
   </thead>
   <tbody>
      <tr> <td>Harrison</td>   <td>George</td>   </tr>
      <tr> <td>Lennon</td>   <td>John</td>   </tr>
   </tbody>
</table>
```

The table is defined inside the `<table>` ... `</table>` tags. The opening `<table>` in this example has two attributes —`border` and `width`. The `border` attribute specifies the width of the table border lines in pixels. Setting this value to "0" will result in all lines being rendered invisible. The `width` attribute sets the width of the table and is used exactly as in the `<hr>` tag —either specifying a number of pixels or a percentage of the screen width.

The `caption` is an optional element that inserts a text heading directly above the table in the browser window.

HTML differentiates between the head and body of a table. The head should always be specified first, and usually contains a single row of titles for each of the columns of information.

A Table Row (`tr`) is used for formatting the cells of individual rows. All the cells of a row belong between the `<tr>` ... `</tr>` tags of that row. Within a row we have cells —the smallest units of table information. There are two types of cell, `th` (Table Header) cells which are used in the table head to give a title to each column, and `td` (Table Data) cells which usually contain the actual information. `th` and `td` are actually interchangeable, except that `th` elements are by default aligned to the centre of the cell and are bolded, while `td` elements are in normal text and are aligned to the left. The alignment of `th` or `td` cells can be changed by using the `align=...` attribute which takes values of `left`, `right`, `center` or `justify` (both `left` and `right` at the same time). We can also set the alignment for an entire row by including the `align=...` attribute in a `tr` definition.

1.5.2 More Complex Table Structures

There are a number of ways in which the basic table specified above could be extended. In particular, we can employ more advanced formatting and cell merging techniques. We examine each of these in more detail in the following sections.

1.5.2.1 Advanced Table Formatting

In the basic **table** tag of Figure 1.11 we saw the **border** and **width** attributes. In addition, we might consider using some of the following.

The **cellspacing** and **callpadding** attributes specify the number of pixels between cells in the table. The value assigned for **cellspacing** controls the number of pixels between cell borders, while **cellpadding** specifies the distance in pixels between the border and the cell content. Figure 1.12 illustrates the difference between **cellspacing** and **cellpadding**.

Figure 1.12
Cell Padding and
Spacing

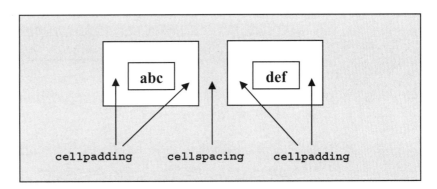

We can format cells by using attributes such as **bgcolor** (background colour), **align** and **width** —all of which we have met before in various other tags. We may now also introduce the rather obvious **valign** (Vertical ALIGNment) tag which takes values of "**top**", "**middle**" or "**bottom**".

However, we can also take advantage of the nature of tables by formatting columns in groups as illustrated in Figure 1.13. It is good style to make use of this technique, since it provides the browser with all the formatting information for the table before the data is presented.

Figure 1.13
Formatting Columns

```
<table border="1" align="center">
   <caption>Formatting Columns</caption>
   <colgroup>
      <col width="50" align="center">
      <col span="3" bgcolor="yellow" width="100"
           align="left">
      <col align="right">
   </colgroup>
   <thead>
      <tr>
         <th>Day</th><th>A</th><th>B</th><th>C</th>
         <th>Total</th>
      </tr>
   </thead>
   <tbody>
      <tr>
         <td>One</td><td>1</td><td>4</td><td>7</td>
         <td>12</td></tr>
      <tr>
         <td>Two</td><td>2</td><td>5</td><td>8</td>
         <td>15</td></tr>
      <tr>
         <td>Three</td><td>3</td><td>6</td><td>9</td>
         <td>18</td></tr>
   </tbody>
</table>
```

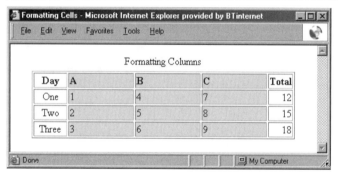

The **colgroup** tag allows us to specify the appearance of each column of the table in turn. Where consecutive columns have similar characteristics, they can be grouped together by the **span** attribute so that a single definition will set out the rule for the display of all like columns.

In the example above, the table consists of 5 columns. From the **colgroup** tag we can see that the first column is 50 pixels wide and is aligned to the centre. Columns 2, 3 and 4 (the next **span** of 3 columns) share a yellow background, are each 100 pixels wide, and are all aligned to the left. The final column is aligned to the right.

1.5.2.2   Cell Merging

Cell merging provides us with much more flexibility in table design because it allows us to specify single cells that span across multiple rows and columns. For example, consider the table architecture of Figure 1.14 below, where a picture might be displayed in Cell 1, with some associated text presented in columns in Cells 2-5.

Figure 1.14
Cell Merging

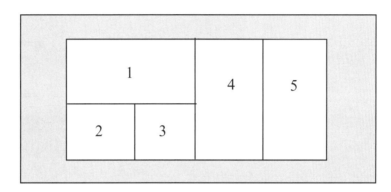

The first task in implementing this table in HTML is to notionally extend all cell lines to the border of the table. This gives a very clear picture of the exact row and column architecture of the table. Figure 1.15 illustrates this process for our example table.

Figure 1.15
Extended Cells

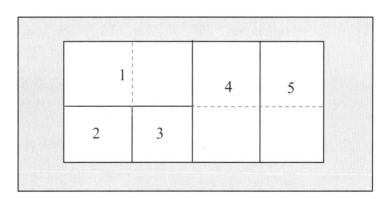

It can be easily seen from Figure 1.15 that cell 1 spans two columns on the same row, while cells 4 and 5 each span two rows within a single column. We can now implement this table in HTML using the **rowspan** and **cellspan** attributes as described in Figure 1.16.

Figure 1.16
Complex Table
Structure

```
<table border="1" width="50%">
    <caption>A Complex Table</caption>
    <colgroup>
        <col       span="4"       width="25%"       align="left"
    valign="top">
    </colgroup>

    <tbody>
        <tr> <td colspan="2" ALIGN="centerv>Cell 1</td>
             <td rowspan="2">Cell 4</td>
             <td rowspan="2">Cell 5</td>
        </tr>
        <tr> <td>Cell 2</td>
             <td>Cell 3</td>
        </tr>
    </tbody>
```

In this table, the `<colgroup>` tag determines that all four virtual columns have 25% of the available table space (which is itself 50% of the horizontal browser space) and that the cells are horizontally aligned to the left and vertically aligned to the top.

The rule for defining merged cells is that the cell is described only in the first row in which it appears. Hence, the first `<tr>` tag contains `<td>` definitions for Cell 1, Cell 4 and Cell 5; while the second `<tr>` tag contains definitions for Cell 2 and Cell 3.

1.6   Page Structures Using Frames

All of our web pages so far have been designed to take over the entire browser window. Using Frames, we have the ability to display multiple pages at a time in separate portions of the browser. Frames, when used properly, can make your site more visually appealing and easy to navigate; but when used carelessly, they can perform untold damage to your user interface. Figure 1.17 illustrates the definition of two frames, arranged in equal areas on the left and right of the browser window.

Figure 1.17
Frame Structures

```
<html>
<head>
     <title>Two Frames</title>
</head>

<frameset cols="50%,50%">
     <frame name="frame1" src="page1.html">
     <frame name="frame2" src="page2.html">
</frameset>
</html>
```

The **<frameset>** tag replaces the **<body>** tag in the HTML page and determines (i) whether the page is to be divided horizontally (**rows**) or vertically (**cols**), (ii) how many divisions there are, and (iii) the amount of the screen taken up by each division. In the example above, the browser window is divided vertically, resulting in 2 frames, each occupying exactly half of the browser space.

The number of comma-separated quantities in the **cols** or **rows** attribute determines the number of divisions. For example, **rows="25%,25%,25%,25%"** would denote 4 frames arranged vertically (in 4 rows), each covering 25% of the browser area. If the quantity is expressed as a raw value (i.e. not as a percentage value) then it denotes the height (or width) of the area in pixels.

Within the **frameset** tag, we have as many **frame** tags as there are rows (or columns) in the frame. Each frame tag has a **name** attribute (for linking, as explained later) and a source (**src**) attribute which identifies the web page to be loaded into that frame. In the example above, the two frames are called "**frame1**" (taking its content from "**page1.html**" and "**frame2**" (refreshed from "**page2.html**").

1.6.1   Nested Frameset Tags

A single `frameset` tag can only divide the browser area into either rows or columns. For more complex arrangements, we must use nested tags as described in Figure 1.18.

Figure 1.18
Nested Framesets

```
<frameset rows="60,*">
        <frame name="header" src="page1.html">

        <frameset cols="120,*">
              <frame name="menu" src="page2.html">
              <frame name="content" src="page3.html">
        </frameset>
</frameset>
```

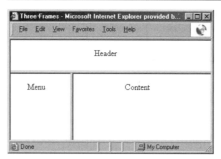

In this example we have a frame arrangement where the browser is split first into two rows (the first `<frameset>` tag) and the second row is further subdivided into two columns (the second `<frameset>` tag). In each case, the division stipulates that the first row/column should occupy a fixed area (60 and 120 pixels respectively) and that the second row/column should occupy the remaining space (the "*****" attribute value).

1.6.2 Frames and Hyperlinks

The purpose of the **name** attribute in a **<frame>** tag is to identify that frame, thereby enabling us to load material into a named frame. For example, the HTML

```
<a href="goHere.html" target="content">
```

would, when clicked, cause the HTML page **"goHere.html"** to be loaded into the frame with the **name** "content".

There are also a number of predefined values that can be used for the **target** attribute as follows.

target="_blank"   loads the page in a new browser window

target="_self"   loads the page into the current frame or window

target="_parent"   loads the page into the parent **<frameset>** (whatever portion of the browser it occupies)

target="_top"   loads the page into the current browser window, overriding any frame definitions.

target="myName"   loads the page into the new window called **"myName"**. This is a good way of ensuring that no more than one browser window is opened in addition to the current one.

1.7 Embedded Media Objects

All of our examples so far have demonstrated how text content can be formatted for presentation on the Web. In this section, we illustrate how other media elements such as images, audio and even video can be incorporated in order to provide a richer experience for the viewer.

1.7.1 Images

HTML supports the inclusion of images on web pages by the `<img>` tag, as illustrated by Figure 1.19.

Figure 1.19
Using Images

```
<html>

<head>
  <title>Images</title>
</head>

<body>
  <h1>The Author</h1>
  <img src="photo.gif" border="0" width="150"
      height="300" alt="A picture of the author">
</body>

</html>
```

In this example, we specify that an image file "photo.gif" is to be placed on the page. The size of the image on the page is specified by the optional **width** and **height** attributes, while the **border** attribute controls the width in pixels of the image frame. The **alt** attribute specifies alternate text to be used if the browser is unable to display the image. The value of this attribute is also used by many browsers to generate a *tooltip* when the viewer's cursor is located on top of the image.

If `width` and `height` attributes are omitted, then the picture will be displayed at its full original size. It is a good idea, however, to specify both `width` and `height` even if the full original size is desired, since most browsers render images after other text content has been loaded. Where the dimensions of images are explicitly specified in the HTML, then the browser knows how much space to leave to accommodate the image.

Where `width` and `height` are specified, but do not match the original image dimensions, then the image will be displayed at the size specified. Beware though, that the two dimensions of the image are scaled independently, so a request that an originally square image (say 100 x 100 pixels) is displayed with `width=80` and `height=50` will result in the image appearing stretched in the browser. For this reason, it is common to find only one dimension (e.g. `width`) specified where image scaling is required. The dimension omitted (`height` in this instance) will be automatically scaled to the same degree.

Images can be incorporated in any part of a web page —for example within paragraphs, table cells or lists. In addition, an image can be used as the anchor (clickable link) in a hyperlink —as illustrated in Figure 1.20.

Figure 1.20
An Image as an
Anchor

```
<a href="aboutMe.html">
   <img src="photo.gif" width="100" height="150"
        border="0" alt="A picture of the author">
</a>
```

1.7.1.1   Image Maps

The previous example illustrates how an image can be used as an anchor to link to other pages on the internet. **Image Maps** provide a means by which a single image can link to many different pages, depending on the area of the image that is clicked.

Image Maps are defined by the `<map>` tag that includes a number of `<area>` tags, each of which defines an area of the image and a destination to be achieved if a click is performed within that area.

The most common **`<area>`** shapes are **`rect`**, **`poly`**, and **`circle`** as defined below.

`rect` takes 4 values corresponding to a pair of (x,y) coordinate values which define the bounding box of a rectangle. For example, the values 1, 1, 100, 150 describe the rectangle between coordinate position (1, 1) and position (100, 150).

`poly` creates a polygon with vertices on the points described by the values given. For example, the values 10, 15, 50, 20, 100, 80, 30, 70 describe the polygon enclosed by the points (10, 15), (50, 20), (100, 80) and (30, 70).

`circle` requires 3 values corresponding to the centre of the circular area and its radius in pixels. For example, the values 100, 140, 20 describe a circular area centered on the point (100, 140) and with a radius of 20 pixels.

Figure 1.21 illustrates the definition of an Image Map.

Figure 1.21
Image Map
Definition

```
<map name="ImageMap">

    <area href="page1.html" shape="rect"
          coords="1, 1, 100, 150" alt="Go to Page 1">
    <area href="page2.html" shape="poly"
          coords="210, 10, 250, 50, 300, 100, 230, 80"
          alt="Go to Page 2">
    <area href="page3.html" shape="circle"
          coords="50, 250, 50" alt="Go to Page 3">
</map>



<img src="image.gif" alt="This is a clickable Image Map"
     usemap="#ImageMap">
```

1.7.2   Video

Many video formats are in common use on the web, including MPEG, AVI, QuickTime, RealVideo and Shockwave. The ability of the browser to deal with these formats depends on the media players available on the client machine.

The `<img>` tag can also be used to embed a video clip into a web page, by specifying the source for the video in the `dynsrc` (dynamic source) property, as illustrated by Figure 1.22, which displays the video file "filmClip.avi".

Figure 1.22
Embedded Video

```
<html>

<head>
     <title>Video</title>
</head>

<body>
  <h1>Watch the video</h1>
  <img dynsrc="filmClip.mpg" start="fileopen" loop="1">
</body>

</html>
```

The operation of the video is controlled by the attributes `start` and `loop`.

Attribute `start` controls when playback should begin, and takes one of 2 values: `fileopen` , which starts playback as soon as the page has loaded; and `mouseover`, which starts playback the first time the user moves the mouse cursor over the area.

Attribute **loop** controls the number of times the complete sequence should be played. A value of –**1** determines that the sequence should play continuously as long as the page is being viewed, while any positive integer indicates the exact number of plays. Any other value (i.e. 0, or a negative value other than –1) will result in the clip being played exactly once.

One very useful property of the **<img>** tag is that when both **src** and **dynsrc** attributes are specified, then **dynsrc** takes precedence —with **src** only used if the client browser is unable to display the **dynsrc** content. This can be used to present video content to those users who are able to process it, with a still image offered as an alternative for others.

Using the **dynsrc** attribute of the **<img>** tag to specify video is attractive in its simplicity, but it should be noted that it is currently only supported by Internet Explorer, and is not part of the W3C standard for HTML.

1.7.2.1 Using **<embed>**

The **<embed>** tag was originally developed by Netscape as a means to include external media items on web pages. Although the tag was not adopted into the HTML standard, it remains supported by most browsers (including Internet Explorer). Figure 1.23 illustrates the use of the **<embed>** tag. The resulting web page is the same as illustrated in Figure 1.22.

Figure 1.23
Using **<embed>**

```
<h1>Watch the video clip</h1>
<embed src="filmClip.avi" height="150" width="130"
                    autostart="true" loop="false">
</embed>
```

With embed, the presentation of the video is controlled by parameters as follows:

height, width   the dimensions of the screen area occupied by the embedded player.

autostart   set to **true** if the video is to run immediately the page has loaded, or **false** if the video is to be started in response to a mouse click from the user.

loop　　　　set to **true** if the video is to repeat continuously, or **false** if it is to play once only.

1.7.2.2　Web Standard Support for Embedded Video

The HTML standard published by the W3C (World Wide Web Consortium) does not recognize either the **dynsrc** or **<embed>** methods for embedding external media items. Instead, they recommend using a generic **<object>** tag to reference all external items; whether audio, video or executable (e.g. applets). The **<object>** tag was first proposed by Microsoft to support Active-X components, and we will examine its use in this context in Chapter 5. However, current browser support for using **<object>** to embed video is not fully realised, so we will not consider it here.

1.7.3　Audio

As for video, there are a large number of audio file formats in common use. Among the most popular are MIDI, MP3, RealAudio and WAV.

The simplest way to include sound on a web page is to make the audio file the target of a hyperlink, as illustrated by Figure 1.24. When the user clicks on the hyperlink, the client's audio player is activated, and the sound is played.

Figure 1.24
Embedded Audio

```
<a href="sound.wav">Click to hear the sound</a>
```

The technique presented in Figure 1.24 is attractive for presentations where we wish to associate a sound with a particular element on the page. By wrapping the element within **<a>** ... **</a>** tags, and specifying the appropriate sound file as the destination of the hyperlink, then we can have the sound played in response to a mouse click on the object.

27

Sometimes, we may wish to embed the sound player on the web page. We can achieve this by using the **embed** tag introduced in Section 1.7.2.1 and specifying the size of the footprint of the media object's control panel. Figure 1.25 demonstrates the specification of an embedded audio player with a width of 300 pixels.

Figure 1.25
Embedded Audio
Player

```
<html>
<head>
      <title>Audio</title>
</head>

<body>
  <h1>Embedded audio player</h1>
  <embed src="music.mid" width="300">
  </embed>
</body>
</html>
```

1.7.3.1   Background Audio

Some web applications require that a background audio track be played automatically when the page loads. This can be achieved by using the **<embed>** tag of the previous example, and setting the **autostart** attribute to **true**. It might also be desirable in such applications to hide the player from view, by setting the **hidden** attribute of the **<embed>** tag to **true**.

The same effect can also be achieved in a more elegant way by the **<bgsound>** element, supported by Internet Explorer, and illustrated in Figure 1.26.

Figure 1.26
Background Audio

```
<head>
      <bgsound src="music.mid" loop="1">
</head>
```

The `<bgsound>` element should be located within the head of the HTML document, and is controlled by the attribute `src` (the address of the audio file to be played) and `loop`. The value of the `loop` attribute determines the number of times the audio should be played. If `loop` is set to −1 (the default) then the audio loops continuously until the user views a different page or presses the browser's stop button. Any other negative value, or zero, will cause the audio file to be played once.

SUMMARY

- HTML is a text-based notation for the specification of content and layout of web pages.
- Structure and layout information is described by markup tags, which are integrated with the page content in the document source.
- The source code is interpreted by a browser that displays the content in accordance with the information contained in the tags.
- Text can be organised into paragraphs, with headings of variable emphasis.
- A range of list structures facilitates the presentation of related data items.
- Pages may be linked by specifying a piece of text (or some other page element) that acts as an anchor. When the anchor is clicked, the browser loads the named destination page.
- A table structure allows us to present statistical information in a logical, structured way.
- Frames provide us with a way to divide the browser area into a number of regions, with a different web page presented in each.
- HTML supports the inclusion of images on web pages. Images can be resized (and re-shaped) dynamically by the browser.
- The HTML standard has not fully specified the integration of audio and video components into web pages. However, each of the major browser providers has implemented its own solution.

FURTHER INFORMATION

http://www.w3.org/TR/html4/
HTML 4.01 specification from the World Wide Web Consortium

http://www.w3schools.com/html/default.asp
Interactive tutorials and examples from W3Schools

http://www.davesite.com/webstation/html/
An interactive tutorial

http://hotwired.lycos.com/webmonkey/authoring/html_basics/
An introduction to HTML from WebMonkey

http://www.2kweb.net/html-tutorial/
HTML tutorial from 2K Communications

http://www.activejump.com/
Wide range of interactive illustrated examples in all aspects of HTML

http://werbach.com/barebones/
List of every tag in the HTML standard, plus the most common Microsoft and Netscape extensions

http://www.anybrowser.org/campaign/
The aim of the "Viewable in any browser" campaign is to promote web accessibility

EXERCISES

1. Implement each of the code examples provided in the text. Try modifying various attributes in each example until you are comfortable with their operation.

2. Build a simple web page that presents your name in one of the heading styles, followed by a paragraph of information about your interests.

3. Extend the web page of Exercise 2 above, by adding additional information organised as lists and tables.

4. Construct a web page that uses embedded images, audio, video, and text to present a multimedia description of some event or technique.

5. One of the most important aspects of multimedia on Web pages is to promote accessibility of the pages to all users regardless of ability or disability. Show how you could use embedded audio objects to provide a service for dyslexic users by having text elements read to the user when requested.

6. Build a collection of related web pages for some business, club or other organisation. Group related information on each page, and provide access to other pages by a menu of hyperlinks.

7. Compare the use of tables and frames as layout mechanisms for the website of Exercise 6 above. What are the main advantages and drawbacks of each approach for the developer, and for the user?

Cascading Stylesheets

In this chapter, we address the following key questions.

- How can we use stylesheets to impose a look and feel on a website?
- How can we control the colour and size of text elements?
- How can we control the appearance of a collection of web pages with a single stylesheet?
- What units of measurement are available?
- How can we control colours and backgrounds on page elements?
- How can we control the spacing between elements?
- How can we apply style to groups of elements?
- How are conflicting style definitions resolved?
- How can we control the position of elements on web pages?

2.1   Introduction to Cascading Stylesheets

Cascading Stylesheets (CSS) allow us to specify the appearance of page elements (colours, spacing, margins, etc.) separately from the structure of our document (headers, body text, links, images etc.).

This separation makes it much easier to manage the appearance of our website.

This chapter should not be regarded as a definitive guide to style properties —rather, the aim is to illustrate the most widely used features of CSS and to lay the foundation for the interactive and animated content to come.

2.1.1   What is Style?

A web page can be described as a combination of *style* and *content*.

Content is the collection of information presented on the page, consisting of paragraphs, headings, lists, images and other elements. Essentially, the content is the information presented on the page — without specifying and details of its presentation.

Style is the description of how the content is to be displayed. For example, we might determine that `<h1>` elements are displayed in the *TimesNewRoman* font, using blue, italicised text on a yellow background. Any style attributes not explicitly specified (e.g. text size in this case) will be displayed using the browser default. We might also specify an element's position, size, shape or any other property of its visual representation.

2.1.2   What is a Stylesheet?

A stylesheet is that section of a web page where style information is described. The information might be associated explicitly with the element to which it applies, it might be gathered together in the head of the document, or it might be placed in an external file and linked to whatever web pages are to be affected.

2.2   Specifying Style Information

There are three methods of specifying style attributes as described in the following sections. These sections also introduce some of the more commonly used style elements.

2.2.1 Inline Style Definitions

Figure 2.1 illustrates *inline* style definition, where the appearance of an element is described using its `style` attribute.

Figure 2.1
Inline Style Definition

```
<p>Text in the default style</p>

<p style="font-size: 20pt">
   Some more text</p>

<p style="font-size: 15pt; color: red">
   Even more text</p>
```

This code results in the three lines of output presented in the image above.

1. The first line, with no style information specified, will appear in the browser default colour, font and size.

2. In the second line, the **style** property of the paragraph specifies that it should be rendered using 20-point text. All other text attributes will be displayed using browser defaults.

3. The third line of output will be displayed in red, using 15-point text, as determined by the `font-size` and `color` style attributes. Any number of style attributes can be set for an element by separating the style definitions by semicolons.

2.2.2 Using the `<style>` Element

Inline style definitions are easy to use and understand, but they must be defined for each element to which they are applied. A better approach is to define global style rules in the head of the document and then to refer to these rules in the element when required. This approach is illustrated in Figure 2.2.

Figure 2.2

Using the `<style>`

Element

```
<html>

<head>
    <style type="text/css">
        p     { font-family: Arial; text-indent: 1cm }
        em    { background-color: yellow }
        .red { color: red }
    </style>
</head>

<body>
    <h1 class="red">First Heading</h1>
    <p>Here is the first paragraph</p>

    <h1>Second Heading</h1>
    <p class="red">Here is the <em>second</em> paragraph</p>
</body>

</html>
```

The `<style>` element in the head of the document is the container for the stylesheet. The `type="text/css"` attribute specifies that what follows is a set of style definitions.

The body of the stylesheet contains the CSS *rules* for this document. Rules are declared in this instance for the `<p>` and `<em>` tags so that all instances of `<p>`, and `<em>` in the document will be displayed in the stated manner. A style *class* named "red" is also defined. Class declarations are preceded by a dot and are applied only when the element is declared as being of that particular class - as in the first heading and the second paragraph from Figure 2.2.

The effect of this stylesheet can be shown by considering each of the elements in the body of the page in turn.

1. The first `<h1>` element is displayed in red, as determined by the `.red` class definition.

2. The first `<p>` element is displayed in the *Arial* font and is indented by 1cm (as per the `style` definition).

3. The second `<h1>` element is displayed in the default style, as no style information is specified for `<h1>`, and no style class is applied.

4. The second `<p>` element is displayed in the Arial font, indented by 1cm as specified in the style definition. The application of the class definition also determines that the text is presented in red. In addition, the text within the `<em>` element is displayed in italics (the default behaviour of `<em>`) on a yellow background (defined in the `style` definition).

2.2.3 Linking External Stylesheets

The third method of specifying style sheet information is to use a separate stylesheet file, which is linked to the HTML document. This is the most flexible of the three methods discussed, as it allows us to use a single style sheet definition across multiple web pages. In addition, a single change to the CSS file will be reflected immediately in all pages to which the file is linked.

Figure 2.3 shows the format an external CSS file while Figure 2.4 illustrates how to connect this CSS file to a HTML document.

Figure 2.3
External Stylesheet
File (styles.css)

```
h1   { color: red }
p    { font-size: 10pt; color: navy }
li   { text-indent: 1cm }
```

Figure 2.4
Using an External
Stylesheet

```
<html>

<head>
    <link rel="stylesheet" type="text/css"
          href="styles.css">
</head>

<body>
    <h1>My Pets</h1>
    <p>A list of my pets, demonstrating a LINKed
       stylesheet</p>
    <ul>
        <li>Cat</li>
        <li>Hamster</li>
        <li>Fish</li>
    </ul>
</body>

</html>
```

The stylesheet is linked to the HTML page by the **<link>** tag,
which has attributes **rel** (relationship —in this case "stylesheet"),
type ("text/css" as used in the **<style>** element earlier) and **href**
(the path/name of the external CSS file). The effect of the stylesheet
is to specify the colours to be used for the **h1** and **p** elements, the
font size of the **p** element, and the indentation of each **li** element.

2.3   CSS Units of Measurement

CSS provides a rich set of units of measurement with which the various dimensions of elements can be specified. These can be categorised as relative units, where size is specified as relative to another size quantity; and absolute units, which are more useful when only the physical dimensions of the display medium are known. Relative units are generally preferable to absolute, since they are more easily and accurately transferable between different media, such as from browser screen to printed page.

2.3.1   Relative Units

The main relative units are **em** (relative to the size of the current font) and **px** (number of pixels, related to the physical dimensions of the viewing device).

The **em** unit is expressed as a multiple of the currently active font size, so that the style rule

```
line-spacing: 1.5em
```

specifies that line spacing should be 30% greater than the default line spacing value. Hence, if the current font size is 12pt, then 1.5em would result in a font size of 18pt.

The **px** unit specifies the number of pixels in the measurement, so that the style rule

```
text-indent: 10px
```

specifies that the first line of a text block should be indented by 10 pixels.

2.3.2   Absolute Units

Absolute units of measurement are quantities that are expressed independently of any physical characteristics of the display media. CSS provides the following absolute units

cm	centimetres
mm	millimetres
in	inches
pt	points
pc	picas

Points and picas are measurements most commonly used in typesetting. CSS specifies that 1 point is equivalent to 1/72 of one inch, while 1 pica is equal to 12 points.

2.4 Text Styles

Cascading Stylesheets afford the web designer a great degree of flexibility in how text is presented on a web page. The following sections illustrate some of the possibilities.

2.4.1 Text Properties

A range of style properties controls the organisation of text blocks on the web page.

The **text-indent** property enables us to specify the amount of indentation on the first list of a text block. The amount of indention can be specified using any of the relative or absolute measurements previously introduced; or as a percentage of the width of the element to which the style is being applied.

The **text-align** element describes the justification option required. It takes one of 4 values: **left** (the default case) for text aligned down the left hand edge; **right** for text aligned down the right hand edge; **justify** for both left- and right-alignment; or **center** when each line of text is to be centred in the display area.

Figure 2.5 illustrates **text-indent** and **text-align** properties applied to paragraph elements.

The appearance of a text block is controlled by the **text-decoration** property, which provides a range of physical characteristics including **underline**, **overline**, **line-through** and **blink**. The default value that specifies plain text with no decoration is **none**.

Figure 2.5
Text Indentation and
Alignment

```
<p style="text-indent: 1cm; text-align:left">
The text-indent property allows us to specify the degree
of indentation on the first line of the block.  A range of
units of measurement are available.  The text-align
property controls the justification of the text block.
</p>

<p style="text-indent: 200px; text-align:justify">
The text-indent property allows us to specify the degree
of
indentation on the first line of the block.  A range of
units of measurement are available.  The text-align
property controls the justification of the text block.
</p>
```

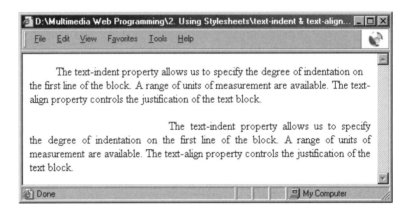

Figure 2.6 illustrates the `text-decoration` property applied to a selection of heading elements.   The spacing between words and letters can also be controlled using CSS properties. The `word-spacing` and `letter-spacing` properties allow us to specify the additional space to be inserted between words and between individual letters respectively. If spacing is to be reduced, then negative values are specified.

Figure 2.6
Text Decoration
Properties

```
<h1 style="text-decoration: underline">
    Underlined text</h1>
<h2 style="text-decoration: overline">
    Overlined text</h2>
<h3 style="text-decoration: line-through">
    Line-through text</h3>
```

Figure 2.7 illustrates a selection of word- and letter-spacing options.

Figure 2.7
Letter and Word
Spacing

```
<p style="letter-spacing: 1.5em">
   Demonstrating letter spacing</p>

<p style="word-spacing: 3cm">
   Demonstrating word spacing</p>

<p style="letter-spacing: -0.1em;
        word-spacing: 1in">
   Both letter spacing and word spacing</p>
```

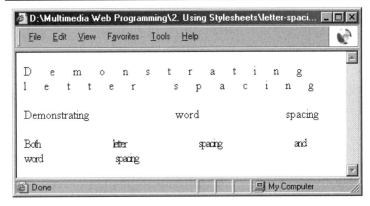

The capitalisation pattern of the text is controlled by the **text-transform** property. This provides three alternative capitalisation patterns:

capitalize the initial character of each word in uppercase
uppercase   all characters of each word in uppercase

     `lowercase`   all characters of each word in lowercase

Capitalisation effects can be switched off by setting `text-transform` to `none` (the default value).

    Figure 2.8 illustrates the effect of the `text-transform` property.

Figure 2.8
Using the
text-transform
Property

```
<p style="text-transform: capitalize">
      Using the capitalize option</p>
<p style="text-transform: uppercase">
      Using the uppercase option</p>
<p style="text-transform: lowercase">
      Using the lowercase option</p>
```

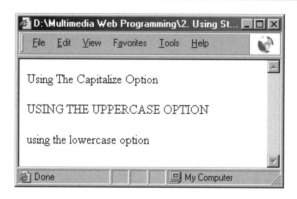

2.4.2   Font Properties

CSS specifies fonts through a selection of font properties that can be individually modified.

    Figure 2.9 demonstrates the `font-family` property, which selects the group ("family") of fonts to be used to render the text. A family is a selection of fonts of similar appearance designed to be used together; where one member of the family is in *italics*, one in **bold**, and so on.

Figure 2.9
Using the
font-family
Property

```
<h1 style="font-family: Arial">Using the Arial font</h1>
<h1 style="font-family: TimesNewRoman">
        Using the TimesNewRoman font</h1>
<h1 style="font-family: Verdana">
        Using the Verdana font</h1>
```

The various members of the font family are selected using the `font-style` and `font-weight` properties —as illustrated in Figure 2.10.

Figure 2.10
The `font-style`
and `font-weight`
Properties

```
<p>Text in the default size, style and weight</p>

<p style="font-style: italic; font-size: 30pt">
    Demonstrating font-style</p>

<p style="font-weight: bold; font-size: 1.5em">
    Demonstrating font-weight</p>
```

The `font-style` property takes properties `italic` or `normal` (the default). The `font-weight` property specifies the density (stroke weight) of the font and takes one of a selection of values as follows:

`100, 200, 300, …, 900:`
an ordered sequence of densities with `100` as the lightest and `900` as the boldest. Font families are not required to implement all 9 options

normal: the default state, equivalent to **400**

bold: equivalent to **700**

bolder: the next highest value in the **100-900** range for which a font family member is available

lighter: the next lowest value in the **100-900** range for which a font family member is available

2.5 Colours and Backgrounds

CSS allows the designer to specify the background of many page elements either as a solid colour or as an image. Where an image is specified then its position on the page and the tiling mechanism used can be controlled.

2.5.1 Colours and Background Colours

The **color** property specifies the colour to be used when rendering text elements. Note again the United States spelling convention (i.e. *color*, not *colour*). There are three ways to specify colour values, as described by the following examples:

color: yellow
> Colour values can be specified using one of the 126 standard colour identifiers

color: rgb(255,255,0)
> The **rgb** function describes colour values by quantities of the red, green and blue primaries —with each primary described in the range 0-255

color: #FFFF00
> Colour values specified as 6-digit hexadecimal values, with each of red, green and blue described as quantities in the range **00** to **FF**

The `backgound-color` property specifies the coloured background of an element. Unlike the `color` property, which applies only to text elements, `background-color` can be applied to any element that occupies browser space; including paragraphs, table rows and cells, headings, and the page body.

Figure 2.11 illustrates the use of the `color` and `background-color` properties.

Figure 2.11
Specifying Colour
Values

```
<head>
<style type="text/css">

    h1     { color: red; background-color: #ffff00 }
    p      { color: rgb(255,255,255);
             background-color: #0000ff }
    body   { background-color: lightgreen }

</style>
</head>

<body>

<h1>Heading</h1>

<p>Paragraph text using the defined colours.
  Note the three different ways in which colour values
  may be defined.</p>
</body>
```

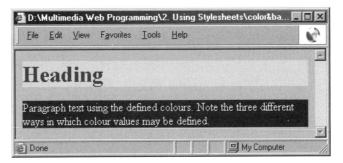

2.5.2 Specifying Backgrounds

Backgrounds can be specified as a colour (by the `background-color` property) or as an image. Background images are controlled by the properties `background-image`, `background-repeat` and `background-position` as follows.

In order to apply a background image to the page, we specify it as

```
background-image: url("picName.gif")
```

If we want the image to be tiled across the page, we can use

```
background-repeat: repeat
```

Options for `background-repeat` are `repeat` (image tiled both horizontally and vertically over the element area), `repeat-x` (image is tiled horizontally only), `repeat-y` (image is tiled vertically only) and `no-repeat` (image not repeated; only one copy of the image is displayed).

We can further control the display of the background image by specifying the position on the page of the first (or only) instance of the image. For example we could align the image to the bottom left corner of the browser by

```
background-position: left bottom
```

The position values can be specified as absolute quantities, percentage values, or as one of `top`, `bottom`, `left`, `right` or `center`.

Figure 2.12 illustrates the use of the background image properties.

Figure 2.12
Using a Background Image

```
<body style="background-image: url(flower.gif);
             background-repeat: repeat-y;
             background-position: top right">

<h1 style="color: red">Hello</h1>

</body>
```

2.6 The CSS Box Model

The CSS Box Model describes the rectangular screen area in which a page element is to be displayed. A number of style attributes control the size and appearance of the box, as well as the positional relationship with the boxes of other elements on the page.

2.6.1 Box Dimensions

The appearance of an element's box is determined by its ***content*** (text, image etc.) and optional ***padding***, ***border*** and ***margin*** areas that surround the content. **Padding** is used to separate the element's content from its **border**, while **margins** serve to provide separation between adjacent page elements. The dimensions of the content area can be controlled by the box `height` and `width` properties. The relationship between these regions is illustrated by the diagram below.

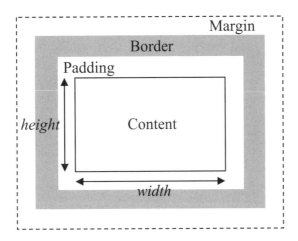

2.6.2   Specifying Margins, Padding and Borders

The recognisable features of margin and padding areas are the width of each area and its colour.

The colour of a *padding* area is the background colour of the element to which the padding property is being applied; while the colour of a *margin* area is the background colour of the element within which the current element is being displayed —usually the body of the web page.

The width of borders and margins can be uniform for all four sides of the box, or can be specified separately for each edge. Figure 2.13 demonstrates a paragraph element with margin and border areas defined. Note how in the case of the margin separate properties **margin-top**, **margin-right**, **margin-bottom** and **margin-left** are specified. Similar properties **padding-left**, **padding-top**, **padding-bottom** and **padding-right** are available for the padding attribute.

Where all four edges are to be specified, it is more convenient to use the form of the attribute demonstrated by the **padding** specification in Figure 2.13. Here the width of all four edges is supplied specified in a single statement; in the order *top*, *right*, *bottom*, *left*. The **margin** property can also be defined in this way.

The second paragraph element in Figure 2.13 also illustrates how the **height** and **width** properties can be used to control the dimensions of the box content area.

Figure 2.13
Margins and Padding

```
<p style="background-color: yellow;
          margin-top:1cm; margin-right:2cm;
          margin-bottom:3cm; margin-left:4cm;
          padding: 10px 40px 10px 40px">
   This paragraph demonstrates the margin and padding
   attributes of the CSS box model.
</p>

<p style="height:100px; width:300px;
          background-color: yellow">
   The gap between the paragraphs illustrates the bottom
   margin property</p>
```

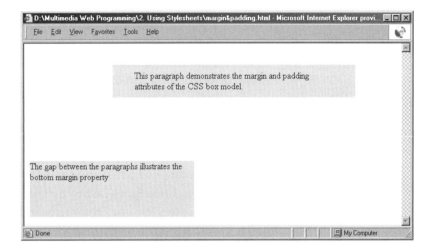

The **margin** and **padding** attributes are sufficiently flexible to enable one, two, three or four values to be specified. Where a single value is provided, such as

```
margin: 10px
```

then it is applied to all four edges. If two values are provided, such as

```
margin: 10px 15px
```

then the top and bottom **margin**s (or **padding**s) are set to the first value, while the left and right regions are set to the second value. If three values are provided, such as

```
margin: 10px 15px 20px
```

then the top is set to the first, the left and right are set to the second, and the bottom is set to the third. If four values are provided, then they are applied to the top, right, bottom and left in order, as illustrated in Figure 2.13.

The **border** of a box is described by its *width*, *colour* and *style*. As for the **margin** and **padding** properties, these can be set individually for each edge, or collectively for the box as a whole.

The width of a box border is described by the properties **border-width**, **border-top-width**, **border-right-width**, `border-bottom-width`, and `border-left-width`. Border width can be set to one of the predefined values `thin`, `medium`, or `thick`; or can be set to an explicit width value (using any of the previously introduced measurements). The `border-width` property is a shorthand mechanism for setting multiple widths in a single statement. As for `margin` and `padding` specifications, one, two, three or four values can be provided.

The colour of a border is specified by the properties `border-color`, `border-top-color`, `border-right-color`, `border-bottom-color`, and `border-left-color`. Any of the three colour specification techniques previously introduced can be applied.

The style of a border is specified by the properties `border-style`, `border-top-style`, `border-right-style`, `border-bottom-style`, and `border-left-style`. The value of border style properties describes the line style in which the border is drawn. A selection from the range of available styles is described in the following list:

`none`	No border. This is equivalent to setting border-width to 0.
`solid`	Border edges drawn as a single straight line segments. This is the default used if no style is explicitly specified.
`dotted`	Border edges drawn as series of dots.
`dashed`	Border edges drawn as series of dashes.
`double`	Border edges drawn as a pair or solid lines where the combined width of the 2 lines and the space between them is equal to the specified border width.
`groove`	A shading affect is used to imply that the border has been etched into the canvas.
`ridge`	The opposite effect to `groove`. A shading effect is used to imply that the border has been raised out of the canvas.

Figure 2.14 illustrates a pair of paragraph objects with varying border properties. The first paragraph has a **thick**, **red**, **ridge** border, applied uniformly to all four edges. The second paragraph specifies information only for the top and bottom borders, leaving left and right at their default state (no border).

Figure 2.14
Border Styles

```
<p style="width=60%;
          background-color: yellow;
          border-width: thick; border-color: red;
          border-style: ridge">
  This paragraph demonstrates the border attributes of
  the CSS box model.
</p>

<p style="width=30%; margin: 2cm;
          border-bottom: 6px green double;
          border-top: 3px blue dotted">
  Setting multiple border properties
</p>
```

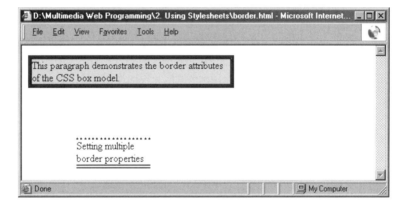

Note the shorthand format used in the second paragraph in Figure 2.14, where border width, colour and style information is specified in a single statement by the style assignment

```
border-bottom: 6px green double
```

This is functionally equivalent to the longer form

```
border-width-bottom: 6px;
border-color-bottom: green;
border-style-bottom: double
```

51

2.7   Applying Style to Grouped and Partial Elements

The style properties illustrated so far have been applied to individual page elements, either through inline specification or through globally specified style rules or class definitions. Sometimes, however, we may want to apply style to a collection of objects while treating the collection as a single object.

The HTML specification provides two options for the specification of *pseudo-elements* – page content that can be treated as a single entity.

The `<div>` and `<span>` tags specify container elements that enclose other page content. They differ in that `<div>` is a block level element, causing a paragraph-style break; while `<span>` is an inline element with no visible characteristics. The `<div>` and `<span>` elements have no further physical representation, but by applying style rules to them, we can create the effect that the elements contained therein are grouped together.

2.7.1   The `<div>` Element

The `<div>` element is a block-level element that is typically used to group related elements on a web page, so that style rules can be applied to the group.

Figure 2.15 illustrates the use of the `<div>` element to place a solid red border around a pseudo-element comprising an image and a paragraph.

Figure 2.15
The `<div>` Element

```
<div style="border: solid red">
    <img src="flower.gif">
    <p>Summertime!</p>
</div>
```

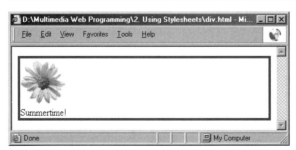

2.7.2 The `<span>` Element

The `<span>` element is an inline element that can be used either to group related elements together (as with `<div>`), or to apply style rules selectively to a portion of a text element. Other than the style rules applied to it, the `<span>` element has no visible effect.

Figure 2.16 illustrates the use of the `<span>` element to apply a background colour selectively to a part of a paragraph element.

Figure 2.16
The `<span>` Element

```
<p>Demonstrating the
    <span style="background-color: yellow">SPAN</span>
    element.
</p>
```

2.8 Resolving Style Conflicts

Style information exhibits properties of inheritance and precedence. Style rules defined for parent elements are also applied to child elements, whereas rules redefined within child elements take precedence over the parent definition. In short, each page element is displayed using the closest available style information. Where no style information is available, then browser defaults are used.

Figure 2.17 illustrates precedence and inheritance by considering three paragraph elements.

The first paragraph will be displayed using the style rules specified for the `<p>` and `<span>` elements in the document `<head>`. No inline style is specified in this case. As the `<span>` element is contained within the `<p>`, then the contents of the `<span>` element will inherit the style rules of the `<p>`, and will be displayed in **blue**, **arial** text on a **yellow** background.

Figure 2.17
Demonstrating
Precedence
and Inheritance

```
<head>
  <style type="text/css">
     p    { font-family: arial; color: blue }
     span { background-color: yellow }
  </style>
</head>

<body>
  <p>Demonstrating <span>inheritance</span> in action</p>

  <p>Specifying
     <span style="font-weight: bold">additional</span>
   style properties</p>

  <p>Demonstrating
     <span style="background-color: lime">
         precedence</span> in action</p>
</body>
```

In the second paragraph, an additional inline style rule is specified for the `<span>` element. This rule adds to the existing inherited rules, so the `<span>` element is displayed in **bold**, **blue**, **arial** text on a **yellow** background.

The additional inline style rule in the third paragraph provides a re-definition of the inherited `background-color` rule. The rule of precedence states that the closest definition takes priority; hence the text in the `<span>` element is displayed in **blue**, **arial** text on a **lime** background.

2.9 Controlling Position

All of the examples so far have assumed that elements are rendered
to the screen in the default top-to-bottom and left-to-right order.
CSS, however, affords much more flexibility over the location of
elements on the page.

2.9.1 Absolute Positioning

Absolute positioning locates objects according to the position
explicitly described by the style properties `top`, `bottom`, `left` and
`right`. For example the style rule

```
position:absolute; top:100px; left: 200px
```

dictates that the upper left corner of the element's box should be
located 100 pixels from the top edge of the display area and 200
pixels from the left edge. In addition, elements located by absolute
positioning are removed from the normal flow and do not affect the
position of subsequent page elements.

Figure 2.18
Absolute Positioning

```
<p style="width: 200;
        border: medium red solid;
        background-color: green;
        color: white;
        position: absolute; top:50; left: 200;
        z-index: 1">
   This element is positioned 200 pixels from the left
   and 50 pixels from the top of the display area
</p>


<p style="width: 200;
        border: medium black solid;
        background-color: blue;
        color: white;
        position: absolute; top:100; left: 50;
        z-index: 2">
   This element is positioned 50 pixels from the left and
   120 pixels from the top of the display area
</p>


<p>This is positioned by the normal top/bottom left/right
   flow</p>
```

55

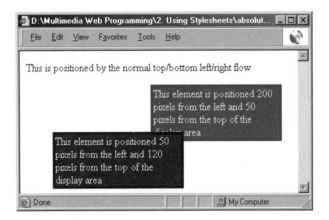

Absolute positioning is illustrated by Figure 2.18, which specifies three paragraph objects, two of which are positioned absolutely. This example also introduces the **z-index** property, which controls the order of placement of overlapping elements, such that those with the highest **z-index** values obscure those with lower values.

2.9.2 Relative Positioning

Relative positioning determines the location of objects as a displacement from their natural position. For example the style rule

> **position:relative; left:10px; top:20px**

dictates that the object's box should be located at a distance 10 pixels to the right (further from the **left**) and 20 pixels below (further from the **top**) than would naturally be the case.

Figure 2.19 illustrates relative positioning by using a **<span>** element to displace a section of a paragraph element by 10 pixels.

Figure 2.19
Relative Positioning

```
<p>Relative
  <span style="position: relative; top: 10px">
  positioning
  </span> in action
</p>
```

56

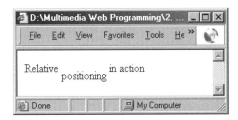

SUMMARY

- Cascading Stylesheets enable us to control the appearance and position of elements on web pages.
- Style information can be specified within individual elements, globally in the document head, or in an external file.
- A range of properties allows us to control the size, style and colour of text elements.
- The size of elements can be specified using a range of absolute and relative measurements.
- Cascading Stylesheets provide control over the colours and backgrounds applied to page elements.
- The CSS Box Model allows us to control the spacing within and between elements.
- The HTML **<span>** and **<div>** elements allow us to apply style to groups of elements or to partial elements.
- Rules for precedence and inheritance provide a framework for the resolution of conflicting style definitions.
- CSS enables us to explicitly control the position of all elements on the web page.

FURTHER INFORMATION

http://www.w3.org/TR/REC-CSS2/
CSS specification from the World Wide Web Consortium

http://www.w3schools.com/css/default.asp
Interactive tutorials and examples from W3Schools

http://www.westciv.com/style_master/academy/css_tutorial/
Free online reference to Cascading Stylesheets

http://www.htmlhelp.com/reference/css/
Collection of CSS links from the Web Design Group

http://www.echoecho.com/css.htm
CSS tutorial from EchoEcho.Com

http://wdvl.internet.com/Authoring/Style/Sheets/
Comprehensive collection of CSS resources

http://www.alistapart.com/articles/practicalcss/
Practical CSS layout tips, tricks and techniques

http://hotwired.lycos.com/webmonkey/authoring/stylesheets/tutorials
/tutorial1.html
Stylesheets tutorial from WebMonkey
http://www.thenoodleincident.com/tutorials/css/
Collection of CSS resources and links

EXERCISES

1. Implement each of the code examples provided in the text. Try modifying various attributes in each example until you are comfortable with their operation.

2. Create an external stylesheet file and link it to a pair of HTML pages. Verify that a single style change in the CSS file causes all linked HTML pages to update when they are reloaded.

3. Produce a web page that illustrates the range of CSS border styles. Provide 6 text boxes, one for each of the `border-style` values, with each having a different `border-color` and `border-width`.

4. Use CSS **absolute** positioning to arrange the position of the text boxes from the previous example. Use the **z-index** property to resolve overlapping elements.

5. Create a single HTML page that combines both inline and embedded CSS styles as follows. All text is contained within either **<p>** or **<h1>** elements. The embedded definition (in the head of the document) should ensure that the default case is that (i) paragraph elements are displayed in the Arial font, using black, 12 point text; and (ii) heading 1 elements are displayed in red, underlined, bolded 16 pt Times Roman text, on a yellow background. In addition, you should demonstrate one exceptional paragraph in blue text, and one exceptional heading in 14 point text on a green background.

6. Create a set of style rules that present headings in red text and represent links as green, italic text with no underline. Apply these style rules to a number of pages.

7. Demonstrate the CSS positioning attributes by producing a web page that comprises three sentences. The first should read "This starts at position (100,100)" and should be positioned at coordinate position (100,100). Similar sentences should be located at coordinate positions (200,200) and (300,300). Use the **<div>** or **<span>** tags to delimit the sentences.

Using Dynamic HTML

CHAPTER OBJECTIVES

In this chapter, we address the following key questions.

- What is Dynamic HTML (DHTML)?
- How does the Document Object Model (DOM) provide a framework for the organization of elements on a web page?
- How does the Document Event Model facilitate dynamic effects in response to user activity?
- How are event handlers specified?
- What types of mouse and keyboard events can be intercepted?
- How can HTML forms be used in DHTML applications?
- What are DHTML filters?
- How can filter parameters be modified dynamically?
- What types of effects can be achieved with filters?

3.1   Introduction to Dynamic HTML

Dynamic HTML (DHTML) allows HTML elements and their attributes to be treated as objects and properties of these objects. Objects and their properties can be then modified by the browser in response to mouse, keyboard or other events, to achieve various effects. Any element or property we have met so far can be dynamically altered in this way. Such processing is known as *client-side scripting*, as the browser on the client machine carries out all computation. Client-side scripting enables a wide range of dynamic effects to be achieved —without the need for costly round-trips to the server to retrieve the next state of the page.

Client-side scripts are usually written in *JavaScript*. In this chapter, we will introduce a few of the most widely used JavaScript structures, but it is not necessary to have a complete understanding of the language in order to develop powerful dynamic pages. A more complete treatment of JavaScript is provided in the following chapter.

3.2 Events and Objects

Dynamic HTML is built around the *Document Object Model* (DOM), and the *Document Event Model*, which provide a naming convention for access of the various objects and properties, and a rich set of actions to which objects can be made to react.

3.2.1 The Document Object Model

The Document Object Model provides a framework within which the elements on a web page are organized. The DOM has two main enabling features:

1. Assignment of identifiers to page elements, so that the element can be directly addressed. For example, the HTML fragment

   ```
   <body>
      <p id=myParagraph>My paragraph</p>
      <img id=myImage src="imageFile.gif">
   </body>
   ```

   defines a pair of objects that can be accessed by the simple dot notation **document.myParagraph** to refer to the paragraph element; and `document.myImage` to refer to the image element.

2. A means of addressing any style property of any element. For example, the foreground colour of the paragraph object above can be referenced by the DHTML expression `document.myParagraph.style.color`.

3.2.2 The Document Event Model

The Document Event Model specifies a number of interactions (events) that can be used to trigger some dynamic activity by the page elements. Various collections of events are available, corresponding to mouse and keyboard action and assorted page activity. The following sections illustrate how these events can be used to affect dynamic change of the appearance on the web page.

3.2.3 Dynamic Modification of Style Properties

We have already seen how Cascading Stylesheets allow us to specify many characteristics of HTML elements. For example, we might specify the style of a paragraph in terms of the character font to be used (CSS property `font-family`), the size of the text (`font-size`), the text and background colours (`color`, `background-color`), and other properties (`text-decoration`, `font-weight`, etc.) The combination of the DOM and the Event Model allow us to modify such properties even after the page has been loaded, in response to events generated by the browser or in response to some action of the user.

Figure 3.1 illustrates dynamic style modification by presenting a paragraph element where the background colour is changed when the user moves the mouse over its box area.

Figure 3.1
Dynamic Modification of Style Properties

```
<html>
<head>
  <title>Dynamic Styles</title>
</head>

<body>
  <span onmouseover="style.backgroundColor='yellow'">
     Welcome to Dynamic HTML
  </span>
</body>

</html>
```

This is an example of *event-driven programming*, where the dynamic operation of the page is specified as an event handler of the form

eventName = "action to be taken"

The event in this case is **onmouseover**, which is automatically generated when the user moves the mouse pointer over the HTML element in question. The action to be taken is to assign a new colour value ('yellow') to the HTML object's **background-color** CSS property. The **style.backgroundColor** notation is an illustration of the DOM naming convention that provides access to any property of any object.

Note that the CSS property (**background-color**) is referred to as **backgroundColor**. This is a general convention in specifying event handlers and is to avoid confusion with the JavaScript subtraction operator (-). Note also, that the CSS property is case-sensitive —i.e. **backgroundColor** rather than *BackgroundColor*, *BACKGROUNDCOLOR* or *backgroundcolor*.

We can change multiple style properties at once by separating the actions by semicolons. Hence if we want the **onmouseover** event to trigger a change in both the text colour and the background colour, we can specify

```
onmouseover = "style.backgroundColor='yellow';
               style.color='red' "
```

Note that the colour values are enclosed in single quotes. This is to enable us to specify text values ('yellow' and 'red') while avoiding confusion with the double quotes used to delimit the code contained in the event handler.

3.2.4 Multiple Event Handlers

We often want to specify more than one event handler for a single HTML object. For example, we might want to modify the example from Figure 3.1 so than the background colour of the text changes when the mouse is moved over the object, but that the original colour is restored when the mouse is moved off the object.

This can be achieved by use of the **onmouseout** event, and is illustrated by Figure 3.2.

Figure 3.2
Multiple Event
Handlers

```
<html>
<head>
  <title>Multiple Event Handlers</title>
</head>

<body>
  <span onmouseover="style.backgroundColor='yellow'"
        onmouseout="style.backgroundColor='white'">
        Welcome to Dynamic HTML
  </span>
</body>
</html>
```

64

Figure 3.2 illustrates a pair of event handlers attached to a single HTML element. The `<span>` element now responds to the `onmouseover` event by changing the background colour to *yellow* when the mouse is moved over the object, and responds to the `onmouseout` event by resetting the background colour to *white* when the mouse is moved away from the object.

3.2.5 Mouse Button Clicks

As well as responding to the mouse cursor moving over and off objects, we can also specify event handlers that are triggered when the mouse button is clicked.

Figure 3.3 introduces the `onclick` event, which is generated when the mouse is clicked on an HTML object. We also introduce the `alert()` function, which generates a pop-up window containing a specified message. Message boxes of this type are often used in event-driven applications to provide timely feedback to the user.

Figure 3.3
Mouse Click Events

```
<html>
<head>
  <title>Mouse-click events</title>
</head>

<body>
  <span onclick="alert('You clicked the text')">
      Welcome to Dynamic HTML
  </span>
</body>

</html>
```

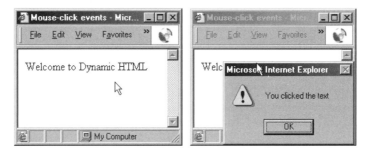

65

3.2.6 Dynamic Modification of HTML Elements

All of the examples so far have illustrated the dynamic modification of style properties of elements within web pages. Dynamic HTML also provides the **innerHTML** and **outerHTML** attributes, which enable us to change any characteristics of an object, or even to replace one object with another.

The **innerHTML** attribute comprises everything between the opening and closing tags of an HTML element. Hence, for the paragraph element

```
<p>This is an example</p>
```

the **innerHTML** property of the element is "*This is an example*". The **outerHTML** attribute has a similar operation, except that it includes the opening and closing paragraph element tags.

Figure 3.4 illustrates the **innerHTML** and **outerHTML** properties by presenting a pair of paragraph elements, each of which has an **onclick** event handler specified. The event handler for the first paragraph causes the **innerHTML** property of the element to be changed, while the event handler for the second paragraph causes the **outerHTML** property of the element to be changed. Note how in the second case, the **outerHTML** property actually changes the element from a paragraph to a Heading1 element —any element can be replaced by any other in this way.

Figure 3.4
Using **innerHTML**
and **outerHTML**

```
<html>
<head>
  <title>innerHTML and outerHTML</title>
</head>

<body>

    <p onclick="innerHTML='I have been clicked!'">
      Click me!</p>

    <p onclick="outerHTML='<h1>I am now a heading!</h1>'">
      I am a paragraph!</p>

</body>

</html>
```

3.2.7 Tracking Mouse Movement

The DHTML Event Model also provides powerful motion tracking facilities, with which we can monitor the position and status of the mouse cursor, and make changes to the appearance of our web page accordingly.

Figure 3.5 illustrates DHTML motion tracking with an example that uses the **onmousemove** event to report the current location of the mouse, and updates the CSS position attributes of an HTML object so that it is relocated to the position of each mouse click.

Figure 3.5
Motion Tracking

```
<html>
<head>
  <title>Motion tracking</title>
</head>

<body onmousemove="coordinates.innerHTML=event.clientX +
                  ',' + event.clientY"
    onclick="movingText.style.left=event.clientX;
            movingText.style.top=event.clientY">
  <span id="coordinates"
      style="position:absolute; top:0; left:0"></span>

  <span id="movingText"
      style="position:absolute; top:100; left:100">
      Mouse clicked here
  </span>

</body>

</html>
```

67

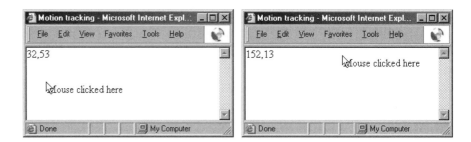

Figure 3.5 represents the most complex example so far, and requires careful study to fully understand its operation.

The page consists of two **<span>** objects:

i)   an empty **<span>**, positioned at the top left corner of the browser; and

ii) a **<span>** containing the text "Mouse clicked here", positioned 100 pixels from the left edge and 100 pixels from the top edge of the browser.

Note that both **<span>** elements are provided with **id** attributes. This assigns to the object a name by which it can be referred. Hence, the first **<span>** can be accessed by the name *"coordinates"*, while the second **<span>** can be accessed by reference to the name *"movingText"*.

In this example, event handlers for **onmousemove** and **onclick** are defined in the **<body>** element. In this way, we specify that we are interested in mouse activity anywhere within the page, rather than within any individual elements.

The role of the **onmousemove** handler is to present the current mouse coordinates within the **<span>** object at the top left corner of the browser window. The current mouse location can be obtained by reading the **clientX** and **clientY** properties of the DHTML **event** object —hence **event.clientX** and **event.clientY**. These values are reported by joining them together with a ',' character, and assigning the result to the **innerHTML** property of the *coordinates* object.

3.3 Defining Scripts

3.3.1 Introducing Scripts

All of our event handlers so far have been specified within the HTML element to which the handler applies. We have also seen how semicolons are used to separate the commands where we wish to specify multiple commands in a single event handler.

Often, we want to use a similar event handler for a number of HTML elements. In these cases, it is attractive to specify the event handler once, and to refer to it on each instance when it is required.

Consider Figure 3.6, which specifies a web page consisting of a pair of **<p>** elements. When the mouse is moved over an element, the **onmouseover** event handler changes the text background colour to yellow; when the mouse is moved away from an element, the **onmouseout** event handler restores the colour to the default white.

Figure 3.6
Similar Event
Handlers

```
<html>
<head>
  <title>Similar Event Handlers</title>
</head>

<body>
   <p onmouseover="style.backgroundColor='yellow'"
      onmouseout="style.backgroundColor='white'">
      Element 1 </p>
   <p onmouseover="style.backgroundColor='yellow'"
      onmouseout="style.backgroundCcolor='white'">
      Element 2 </p>
</body>
</html>
```

69

This example requires that identical event handlers are specified for each paragraph element. A more efficient representation would be to define the event handlers once only, and to refer to them by name when required. We can achieve this by representing the event handlers as *JavaScript* functions.

JavaScript is the language of client-side scripting —defining code that is executed by the browser in response to certain events. Actually, all of the event handlers we have seen so far have also been examples of JavaScript code.

Figure 3.7 presents a recoding of the previous example to implement the event handlers within JavaScript functions.

Figure 3.7

Using JavaScript

```
<html>
<head>
   <title>Using JavaScript</title>

   <script language="JavaScript">

      function highlight() {
         event.srcElement.style.backgroundColor='yellow';
      }

      function lowlight() {
         event.srcElement.style.backgroundColor='white';
      }

   </script>
</head>

<body>
   <p onmouseover="highlight()"
      onmouseout="lowlight()">
      Element 1
   </p>

   <p onmouseover="highlight()"
      onmouseout="lowlight()">
      Element 2
   </p>
</body>

</html>
```

The example of Figure 3.7 illustrates a pair of event handlers presented as JavaScript functions **highlight** and **lowlight**. The functions are enclosed within **<script>** ... **</script>** tags in the head of the web page. (Actually, the `<script>` element can appear anywhere within the page, but it is more usual to locate it within the head.)

In Figure 3.6, we were able to simply say

```
style.backgroundColor='yellow'
```

to change the colour. The browser did not need to be told which element the command applied to, since the event handler was located within the tags for that element. In the corresponding code from Figure 3.7, on the other hand, the browser needs to be explicitly told which object the event handler is to be applied to. The event model property

```
event.srcElement
```

is used to address the object that caused the event, hence the code

```
event.srcElement.style.backgroundColor='yellow'
```

is interpreted as meaning "*set the background colour of the element that caused the event to yellow*"

3.3.2 Conditional Actions

One of the most useful JavaScript structures is the `if` construct, which allows us to specify alternative operations based on some condition. Figure 3.8 illustrates the `if` construct by rewriting the highlight/lowlight example of Figure 3.7 as a single function that checks the current colour of the paragraph text before changing it.

The structure of the `if` construct is

```
if (condition) {
    Statements to be executed if
    the condition is true
}
else {
    Statements to be executed if
    the condition is false
}
```

Note in Figure 3.8 the difference between the use of = (single equals sign) and == (double equals sign). The single equals sign is used to denote assignment (when a value is being assigned to some object), while the double equals sign is used in the comparison for equality.

Hence we have

```
if (event.srcElement.style.backgroundColor=='yellow')
```

to test the value of the attribute and

```
event.srcElement.style.backgroundColor='yellow'
```

to set a new text colour for the element.

Figure 3.8
Conditional
JavaScript

```
<html>
<head>
  <title>Conditional Execution</title>

  <script language="JavaScript">
    function changeColour() {
      if(event.srcElement.style.backgroundColor=='yellow') {
            event.srcElement.style.backgroundColor='white'
      }
      else {
            event.srcElement.style.backgroundColor='yellow';
          }
      }
  </script>
</head>

<body>
    <p onmouseover="changeColour()"
      onmouseout="changeColour()"> Element 1 </p>
    <p onmouseover="changeColour()"
      onmouseout="changeColour()"> Element 2 </p>
</body>
</html>
```

3.4 Working with Forms

HTML Form objects provide a variety of tools that enable the user to provide keyboard and mouse input to a web application. The normal use of forms is to provide interaction in client-server situations, but the ability of DHTML to manipulate forms using the DOM and Event model makes form input elements well suited for use in interactive multimedia applications.

3.4.1 Obtaining Values from Form Fields

HTML form objects provide a very flexible means of obtaining user input for interactive dynamic web applications. Forms provide us with a rich set of input options, including text boxes, drop-down lists, radio buttons and checkboxes; and the current state of all of these is made available for retrieval and modification by the Document Object Model (DOM).

Figure 3.9 presents a simple form containing a single text box and a button object. When the button is pressed, then a message box is generated, reporting the contents of the text box.

Figure 3.9
Using Forms

```
<html>
<head>
  <title>FORMs</title>
</head>

<body>

<form name="myForm">
   Enter your name<br>
   <input type="text" name="myName" size="10"><br>
   <input type="button" value="Click here"
          onclick="alert('hello ' +
                         myForm.myName.value)")
</form>

</body>
</html>
```

73

Figure 3.9 demonstrates that the value of a form field can be accessed by adhering to the naming convention

```
formName.fieldname.value
```

which, for a form with name attribute "myForm" and a field with name attribute "myName" (as in Figure 3.9) gives us the name

```
myForm.myName.value
```

3.4.2   Dynamic Interaction with Forms

Figure 3.10 presents a more advanced example where the background and text colours of a web page are selected through form elements. This example also introduces the **onchange** method, which is generated when the value of a form element is modified.
   Two drop-down lists are used to present the options to the user, and the **onchange** event handler updates the **color** and **background-color** attributes as appropriate. Note particularly how we can access the style properties of the **<body>** element by the DOM reference

```
document.body.style.propertyName
```

The **document** object is the top level of the DOM specification, and provides a "base point" from where all other properties of the page can be accessed.

Figure 3.10
Dynamic Interaction
with Forms

```
<html>
<head>
  <title>Dynamic Operation with FORMs</title>

  <script language="JavaScript">
    function changeColour() {
       document.body.style.backgroundColor=
                                myForm.bgColour.value;
       document.body.style.color=myForm.textColour.value;
    }
  </script>
</head>

<body>

<form name="myForm">
    Choose background colour<br>
    <select name="bgColour" onchange="changeColour()">
        <option value='red'>Red
        <option value='black'>Black
        <option value='blue'>Blue
    </select><br><br>

    Choose text colour<br>
    <select name="textColour" onchange="changeColour()">
        <option value='white'>White
        <option value='yellow'>Yellow
        <option value='green'>Green
    </select>
</form>

</body>
</html>
```

Figure 3.11 illustrates the form *radio button* and *checkbox* elements. Radio buttons are used to select one from a number of mutually exclusive options, while checkboxes allow multiple selections to be made from a collection. Figure 3.11 provides an

interface through which the user can control the appearance of a piece of text. A set of radio buttons is used to select the size of the text, while a set of checkboxes enables the application of a selection of text formatting styles.

Figure 3.11
Other `<form>`
Elements

```
<html>
<head>
   <title>Dynamic Operation with FORMs</title>

   <script language="JavaScript">
     function updateText() {
         if (myForm.textSize[0].checked)
             myText.style.fontSize='12pt';
         else myText.style.fontSize='18pt';

         if (myForm.boldText.checked)
             myText.style.fontWeight='bold';
         else myText.style.fontWeight='normal';

         if (myForm.italicText.checked)
             myText.style.fontStyle='italic';
         else myText.style.fontStyle='normal';

         if (myForm.underlineText.checked)
             myText.style.textDecoration='underline';
         else myText.style.textDecoration='none';
     }
   </script>
</head>

<body>
<span id=myText
     style="color: red; border-style:solid;
             border-width:1; font-size:12pt;
             font-weight:normal; text-decoration:none;
             font-style:none">
     Change the text style</span>
<form name="myForm">
Choose text size<br>
<input type=radio name=textSize checked>Small
<input type=radio name=textSize>Large <br><br>

Choose text style<br>
<input type=checkbox name=boldText>Bold
<input type=checkbox name=italicText>Italic
<input type=checkbox name=underlineText>Underline
<br><br>

<input type=button value=Change onclick="updateText()">
</form>
</body>
</html>
```

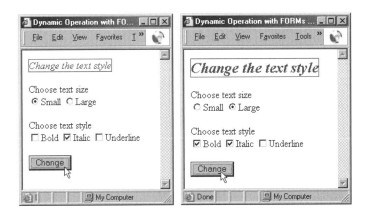

The event handler is contained in a JavaScript function that consists of four **if** statements. The first statement sets the **fontSize** property in accordance with the status of the radio buttons, while the remaining three statements control the *bold*, *italic* and *underline* properties. Note that each element in a set of radio buttons or checkboxes is addressed by an index value, with the first element having an index of 0. Hence, for the set of radio buttons, the *small* option is addressed as **myForm.textSize[0]**, while the large option is addressed as **myForm.textSize[1]**. For each button, the **checked** property returns *true* if the corresponding button has been selected, and *false* if the button is not selected.

3.4.3   Form Validation and Keyboard Events

DHTML applications often use forms as a means of obtaining parameters for animations, or some other input for processing. Where input is entered as text, we often want to validate it to ensure it matches certain criteria. To assist in this, DHTML provides a selection of keyboard events that can be used to intercept key presses and reject them if they are deemed to be inappropriate. For example, Figure 3.12 presents an example where the user is asked to provide his age in a text box. The **onkeypress** event is used to analyse each key pressed, and to reject any that are non-numeric.

Figure 3.12
Form Validation and
Keyboard Events

```html
<html>
<head>
  <title>Validated Text Input</title>

  <script language="JavaScript">
    function verifyKeyPress() {
       var thisKey=event.keyCode;
       if (thisKey<=48 || thisKey>=57)
          event.returnValue=false;
    }
  </script>
</head>

<body>
  <form name="myForm">
  Please enter your age<br>
  <input type=text name=theAge size=3
        onkeypress="verifyKeyPress()"> <br><br>
  <input type=button value=Continue
        onClick="alert('Input accepted: ' +
                       myForm.theAge.value)">
  </form>
</body>
</html>
```

On each key press, the **onkeypress** event passes control to the event handler specified in the JavaScript function **verifyKeyPress()**. In the function, the ASCII code of the key pressed is returned in the **event.keyCode** object, and this value is compared to the acceptable range. If the ASCII code is found to be unacceptable (corresponding to a non-numeric value), then the DHTML object **event.returnValue** is set to *false* —causing any further processing of the element to be abandoned —hence the key pressed will not be displayed in the text box. Note the use of the JavaScript *logical or* (||) operator in the **if** statement. A full set of JavaScript comparison operators is provided later in Figure 4.3.

3.5   Special Effects with DHTML Filters

The CSS Filter property enables us to achieve a wide range of graphical effects on web pages, where all effects are rendered and presented by the browser. All filter properties are programmable, so that the effects can be dynamically controlled in response to user actions.

3.5.1   Using Filters

Figure 3.13 illustrates the definition of CSS filters using the `fliph` and `flipv` filters, which cause web elements to be mirrored either horizontally or vertically.

Figure 3.13
The `fliph` and `flipv` Filters

```
<body>
    <h1 style="position:absolute; top:0; left:0">
        Normal text</h1>
    <h1 style="position:absolute; top:50; left:0;
                filter: flipv">
        Flipped vertically</h1>
    <h1 style="position:absolute; top:100; left:0;
                filter: fliph">
        Flipped horizontally</h1>
    <h1 style="position:absolute; top:150; left:0;
                filter: flipv fliph">
        Both horizontally and vertically</h1>
</body>
```

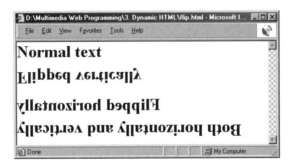

Filters can be applied to any page element as long as the element has a defined height and width. Some objects, such as images and tables, have this by default, but others require that the height or width are explicitly set, or that the object is absolutely positioned.

Note also how multiple filters can be applied in series as in the final example.

3.5.2   Controlling Transparency

DHTML provides a pair of filters that implement transparency effects. The **chroma** filter allows us to remove any colour from an element, while the opacity of entire objects is controlled by the **alpha** filter.

3.5.2.1   Transparency Using the Chroma Filter

The **chroma** filter has two parameters —the *chroma* (colour) to be rendered as transparent (thereby exposing the content behind the object in question), and an *enabled* switch, determining whether the filter is swiched on or off. Figure 3.14 illustrates the specification and application of the chroma filter.

Figure 3.14
*The **chroma** Filter*

```
<body>
    <p style="filter:chroma(color=green, enabled=true);
              font-family:arial; font-size:24pt;
              position:absolute">
        <font color=red>Red</font>
        <font color=green>Green</font>
        <font color=blue>Blue</font>
        <font color=yellow>Yellow</font>
        <font color=black>Black</font>
    </p>
</body>
```

In Figure 3.14, the filter is applied by the CSS code

```
filter: chroma(color=green, enabled=true)
```

in the style definition for the paragraph object. Note how parameters for filters are specified as a series of comma-separated *name=value* assignments.

The paragraph itself contains a selection of text in different colours. As the paragraph is rendered, so the filter is applied, suppressing the display of any pixels where the colour coincides with the filter's `color` parameter —the green text in this example.

3.5.2.2   Transparency Using the Alpha Filter

One of the most frequently used graphical effects is the gradual transition from one page element to another. This is facilitated by the `alpha` filter that enables us to gradually blend foreground elements into the background. The transition is controlled by 3 parameters: the start and finish opacity (density) of the transition, expressed as a percentage; and the style of the transition (1, 2 or 3; where 1=linear, 2=circular, and 3=rectangular). Figure 3.15 illustrates a selection of gradient effects.

Figure 3.15
The `alpha` *Filter*

```
<body>
  <table border=0 cellspacing=5 cellpadding=0
        align=center>
  <tr align=center><td>
    <span style="filter:alpha(opacity=0,
                             finishopacity=100, style=1);
              background-color:blue; width:140;
              height:20"> </span>
    <span style="filter:alpha(opacity=100,
                             finishopacity=0, style=1);
              background-color:blue; width:140;
              height:20"> </span>
  </td></tr>
  <tr align=center><td>
    <img src=photo.gif
        style="filter:alpha(opacity=100,
                             finishopacity=0,style=2)">
  </td></tr>
  <tr align=center><td>
    <span style="filter:alpha(opacity=100,
                             finishopacity=20, style=3);
              background-color:brown; color:white;
              width:280; padding:15;
              font-family:arial; font-size:12pt">
        Gradient styles </span>
  </td></tr>
  </table>
</body>
```

Figure 3.15 presents a table with 3 rows, where each row illustrates one of the transition styles. The top row contains 2 <span> objects with blue backgrounds, each of which encloses a *linear* gradient from 0% to 100% and from 100% to 0% respectively. The net effect is to create a single blue bar, which fades out at the left and right hand sides. The middle row demonstrates the *circular* transition effect applied to an image. The final row contains a <span> object with a *rectangular* gradient used to create a button-like effect around a piece of text.

3.5.3 Text Effects

DHTML provides a range of filters that are most often used to implement various graphical effects on text elements.

3.5.3.1 Adding Shadows

Shadows can be added to text elements by the application of two filters.

The **shadow** filter creates a shadow that fades towards the edges, controlled by 2 parameters. The **direction** property determines the direction in which the shadow is applied, and is expressed as an angular quantity, where 0 represents above, 45 represents above right, 90 represents right, and so on at 45° intervals. The **color** property specifies the colour of the shadow applied to the text.

The **dropshadow** filter creates a shadow with the same sharp edges as the object casting the shadow. The drop shadow is expressed as an offset from the position of the casting object, plus the colour of the shadow.

The **shadow** and **dropshadow** filters are illustrated by Figure 3.16.

Figure 3.16
Text Shadows

```
<body>
  <h1 style="position:absolute; top:30; left:50;
             font-family:arial; font-size:24pt;
             color:black;
             padding: 10px;
             filter:shadow(direction=45,color=red)">
    Demonstrating text shadows
  </h1>

  <h1 style="position:absolute; top:100; left:50;
             font-family:arial; font-size:24pt;
             color:black; padding:10px;
             filter:dropshadow(offX=4,offY=4,color=gray)">
    Demonstrating drop shadows
  </h1>
</body>
```

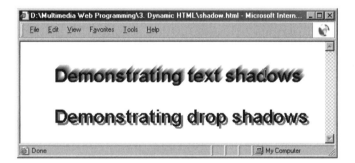

3.5.3.2 Glowing Text

The **glow** filter specifies a coloured aura around a text object. It is controlled by two parameters. The **color** attribute sets the colour of the glow, while the **strength** attribute is a number in the range 0-255 that determines the intensity of the glow (values in the range 0-10 give best results). Figure 3.17 illustrates the operation of the glow filter.

Figure 3.17
Glowing Text

```
<body style="background-color: pink">
  <h1 style="position:absolute; top:100; left:100;
             font-family:arial; font-size:24pt;
             color:black; padding:10px;
             filter:glow(color=red, strength=8)">
      Glowing text
  </h1>
</body>
```

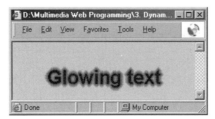

3.5.4   Image Filters

A set of three image filters can be used to apply simple image processing effects to images or text. The **invert** filter applies a negative image effect; the **gray** filter removes all colour from the object, leaving a greyscale representation; and the **xray** filter generates an x-ray effect, which is essentially an inversion of the greyscale representation. Figure 3.18 demonstrates the application of these filters. Note that in a black & white reproduction, the effect of the invert and x-ray filters appears to be identical. The website contains a colour reproduction where the difference is apparent.

Figure 3.18
Image Filters

```
<body>
  <img src=photo.jpg style="filter: gray">
  <img src=photo.jpg style="filter: invert">
  <img src=photo.jpg style="filter: xray">
</body>
```

3.5.5   Motion Filters

The **blur** and **wave** filters are supplied to help create the illusion of motion in static presentations. Either filter can be applied in a variety of directions and some quite convincing effects can be obtained by careful selection of the relevant parameters.

3.5.5.1   The **blur** Filter

The **blur** filter is controlled by 3 properties: **add**, **direction**, and **strength**. The **add** property is a Boolean value, which when true, adds a copy of the original image over the blurred image to create a more subtle effect. The **direction** property is expressed as an angular quantity (as for the **shadow** filter earlier, and determines the direction in which the filter will be applied. The **strength** property controls the density of the blurring effect.

Figure 3.19 illustrates the application of the **blur** filter to a text element (although it can equally be applied to images).

Figure 3.19
*The **blur** Filter*

```
<body>
  <h1 style="position:absolute; top:100; left:100;
             font-family:arial; font-size:24pt;
             color:black; padding:10px;
             filter:blur(add=false, direction=45,
                         strength=7)">
      Blurred text
  </h1>
</body>
```

3.5.5.2 The wave Filter

The **wave** filter allows us to apply *sine wave* distortions to elements on our web pages. This filter is controlled by 4 properties. The **add** property, as for the **blur** filter, is a Boolean value that specifies the presence or otherwise of an original copy of the element. The **freq** property determines the frequency of the sine wave. A higher value for this property creates a more pronounced effect. The **phase** property indicates the *phase shift* of the sine wave. This property is useful for creating a more gentle effect. Finally, the **strength** property controls the amplitude of the sine wave to be applied.

Figure 3.20 demonstrates the application of the **wave** property to a text element.

Figure 3.20
The **wave** *Filter*

```
<body>
    <h1 style="position:absolute; top:100; left:100;
               font-family:arial; font-size:48pt;
               color:black;
               filter:wave(add=false, freq=2, phase=5,
                           strength=8)">
        The wave effect on text
    </h1>
</body>
```

3.5.6 Dynamic Modification of Filter Parameters

All of the filter effects thus far have been specified explicitly as CSS **style** attributes. In practice, however, the most effective use of filters is dynamic, either controlled by some algorithm or modified in response to mouse or keyboard events.

All filter parameters are available to JavaScript code by the notation

$$objectName.\texttt{filters}(\textit{"filterName"}).property$$

For example, for an image with an **id** attribute of "thisImage" and an **alpha** filter applied, we could modify the parameters of the filter by the code

```
thisImage.filters("alpha").opacity=0;
thisImage.filters("alpha").startingopacity=100;
thisImage.filters("alpha").style=1
```

Figure 3.21 presents a version of the **chroma** filter example from Figure 3.14, where the transparent value is selected from a drop-down list.

Figure 3.21
Dynamic Modification of Filter Parameters

```
<head>
   <script language=JavaScript>
      function modifyFilter() {
          chromaDemo.filters("chroma").color=
                      colourForm.colourChoice.value;
      }
   </script>
</head>

<body bgcolor=orange>
   <p id=chromaDemo
      style="filter: chroma(color=green, enabled=true);
             font-family:arial; font-size=24pt;
             position:absolute; top:50">
      <font color=red>Red</font>
      <font color=green>Green</font>
      <font color=blue>Blue</font>
      <font color=yellow>Yellow</font>
      <font color=black>Black</font>
   </p>
   <form id="colourForm">
     <select name=colourChoice onChange="modifyFilter()">
       <option value=red>Hide red</option>
       <option value=green selected>Hide the green</option>
       <option value=blue>Hide the blue</option>
       <option value=yellow>Hide the yellow</option>
       <option value=black>Hide the black</option>
     </select>
   </form>

</body>
```

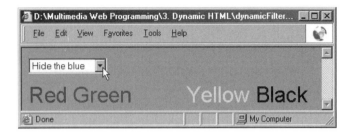

In this example the **form** object *colourForm* enables the user to select the colour value to be used in the **chroma** filter. When the form's **onChange** event is raised, the JavaScript function **modifyFilter** is invoked, which updates the **color** attribute of the paragraph's **chroma** filter to the user's selection.

3.5.7 Transitions

DHTML transitions allow a number of effects to be applied to the appearance and disappearance of page elements. There are 2 transition filters, **blendTrans** and **revealTrans**.

3.5.7.1 Blend Transitions

Figure 3.22 illustrates the use of the **blendTrans** filter. The blend transition is invoked by a call to the **fadeout()** function. This is a three-stage process and is common to all transition operations. First the **apply()** method of the transition is called to initialise the transition for the element. Once this is done, the **visibility** of the element is set to **hidden**. This takes effect when the transition's **play()** method is invoked.

The filter itself is characterised by the duration property that describes the time required for the transition in seconds.

Figure 3.22
Blend Transitions

```
<head>
  <script language=JavaScript>
    function fadeOut() {
      textDemo.filters("blendTrans").apply();
      textDemo.style.visibility="hidden";
      textDemo.filters("blendTrans").play();
    }
  </script>
</head>

<body style="background-color: black">
  <div id=textDemo onClick="fadeOut()"
      style="position:absolute; top:100; left:100;
            font-family:arial; font-size: 24pt;
            color: red;
            filter:blendTrans(duration=2)">
      Click to fade out
  </div>
</body>
```

3.5.7.2 Reveal Transitions

The **revealTrans** filter allows us to use professional-style transitions between objects on web pages. There is a collection of 24 visual transitions available, as described by the following table.

Transition	Effect	Transition	Effect
0	Box In	12	Random Dissolve
1	Box Out	13	Split Vertical In
2	Circle In	14	Split Vertical Out
3	Circle Out	15	Split Horizontal In
4	Wipe Up	16	Split Horizontal Out
5	Wipe Down	17	Strips Left Down
6	Wipe Right	18	Strips Left Up
7	Wipe Left	19	Strips Right Down
8	Vertical Blinds	20	Strips Right Up
9	Horizontal Blinds	21	Random Bars Vertical
10	Checkerboard Across	22	Random Bars Horiz.
11	Checkerboard Down	23	Random

Figure 3.23 illustrates the operation of the **revealTrans** filter. The filter takes 2 parameters —the **duration** in seconds of the transition, and the **transition** number (as presented in the table above). The code which implements the transition is as for the **blendTrans** filter —with calls to the **apply()** and **play()** methods either side of a modification of the object's **visibility** attribute.

Figure 3.23 presents a pair of images that occupy the same location on a page. When the image that is currently on top (with the lowest **z-index**) is clicked, then the random **revealTrans** filter is applied to reveal the other image below.

Figure 3.23
Reveal Transitions

```
<head>
<script language=JavaScript>
   function blend() {
      pic1.filters("revealTrans").apply();
      pic1.style.visibility="hidden";
      pic1.filters("revealTrans").play();
   }
</script>
</head>

<body bgcolor=black>
   <img id=pic1 src=photo.jpg
       style="position:absolute; top:10; left:10;
             z-index:2; visibility:visible;
             filter:revealTrans(duration=10,
                                 transition=23)"
       onClick="blend()">
   <img id=pic2 src=photo.jpg
       style="filter: xray;
             position:absolute; top:10; left:10;
             z-index:1; visibility:visible">
</body>
```

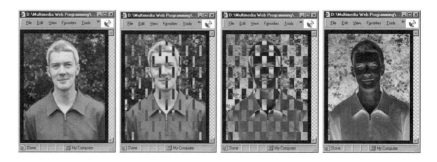

90

SUMMARY

- Dynamic DHTML (DHTML) is a set of technologies that enable us to implement interactive and animated web applications.
- The Document Object Model (DOM) provides access to every style property of each element on a web page.
- The Document Event Model provides a framework for page elements to react to a wide range of user events.
- The action to be taken in response to a named event is specified in JavaScript.
- A wide range of events can be intercepted, including mouse clicks, cursor movement and keyboard activity.
- The HTML form element provides an interface for users to provide input to DHTML applications.
- HTML forms provide a wide range of interaction tools, including text boxes, checkboxes, drop-down lists and radio buttons.
- A wide range of DHTML filters is available to apply image processing effects to page elements.
- All of the parameters of the various filters are available for modification in event handler code.
- Filter effects include motion simulation, image modification, text rendering and transitions between page elements.

FURTHER INFORMATION

http://www.w3.org/DOM/
The World Wide Web Consortium DOM home page

http://www.w3schools.com/dhtml/default.asp
W3Schools DHTML tutorial

http://www.javascriptkit.com/dhtmltutors/domevent1.shtml
Event Handling in the DOM - Tutorial

http://hotwired.lycos.com/webmonkey/authoring/dynamic_html/tutorials/tutorial1.html
Dynamic HTML tutorial from WebMonkey

http://www.brainjar.com/dhtml/events/l
The DOM Event Model

http://www.webreference.com/dhtml/
Collection of Dynamic HTML tutorials from DHTML Lab

http://msdn.microsoft.com/library/default.asp?url=/workshop/author/dhtml/overview/dhtml_overviews_entry.asp
DHTML Tutorials from MSDN

http://www.course.com/downloads/newperspectives/crweb2/dhtml/index.html#dhtml
Selection of DHTML tutorials from Thompson Learning

http://msdn.microsoft.com/library/default.asp?url=/workshop/author/filter/filters.asp
Introduction to DHTML Filters and Transitions – MSDN

http://www.appliedhealthservices.com/personal/Webdesign/DHTMLtext.htm
Examples of DHTML Filters

EXERCISES

1. Implement each of the code examples provided in the text. Try modifying various attributes in each example until you are comfortable with their operation.

2. Create a web page containing a paragraph displayed in 10pt Times Roman font. Add an event handler to this element so that when the element is clicked, the text is displayed in 14pt Arial font.

3. Create a web page with 3 `<span>` elements arranged on separate lines, and with event handlers so that an element is highlighted by changing its background colour as the mouse cursor is passed over it. When the mouse moves off an element, then it should be returned to its normal state.

4. Build an animated menu by converting the `<span>` objects from Exercise 3 into hyperlinks. The menu should provide the user with links to a choice of search engines (e.g. www.google.com, www.altavista.com, www.yahoo.com).

5. Construct a web page where the only element is a single image (of your choice), displayed in the centre of the browser. When the image is clicked, it should be replaced by a second image (of your choice) in the same position.

6. Modify the example in Exercise 5 so that each time the image is clicked, the picture changes: i.e. when the image is clicked the first time, it is replaced with a second image; when the image is clicked a second time, then the first image is re-displayed.

7. Build a web page that presents an image (of your choice) beside a form that enables the user to dynamically modify the attributes of an `alpha` filter applied to the image. The `opacity` and `startingopacity` parameters of the filter should be specified using text boxes, while the `style` parameter should be controlled by a set of radio buttons. The new filter parameters should be applied when the user clicks an "Apply changes" button.

8. Build a web page that presents a `<span>` object containing text displayed in 24pt Times Roman font with a `shadow` filter applied. Provide a form interface that allows the user to select from the 8 possible values for the filter's `direction` property (0, 45, 90, 135, 180, 225, 270, 315).

9. Provide a form-driven version of the example in Figure 3.23, so that the number of the transition type required (0-23) is selected by the user from a drop-down list.

Client-side Programming
with JavaScript

CHAPTER OBJECTIVES

In this chapter, we address the following key questions.

- How can we embed JavaScript code within web pages?
- How can we manipulate variables and perform simple arithmetic and input/output?
- What constructs for iteration and selection are available?
- How are data types handled in JavaScript?
- How are functions defined and used?
- How are arrays defined and manipulated?
- Which language objects are available, and what functions do they provide?
- How can JavaScript be used to program the animation of CSS properties?
- How can interrupts be used to implement timed animation?

4.1 Introduction to Client-side Scripting with JavaScript

Scripting is a form of programming that affords us the opportunity to add functionality and interactivity to our web pages. Scripts are usually executed on the client machine (hence client-side scripting) and are parsed and interpreted by the browser. JavaScript is the most commonly used web scripting language (the main alternative is VBScript —a scripting version of Microsoft's Visual Basic) and has developed into a fully functional programming language suitable for implementing many complex algorithms. Here, we discuss the main elements of the JavaScript language and demonstrate how JavaScript code is embedded into web pages.

First, we introduce the JavaScript language and present the basic input and output operations that enable us to implement interactive solutions within Web pages. We also introduce variables and comparison operators.

4.1.1 A First JavaScript Program

Figure 4.1 presents a simple JavaScript program, and demonstrates how it is embedded within a web page. The program is the traditional "Hello World" application that outputs a text message on the display device.

Figure 4.1
A First JavaScript
Program

```
<html>
<head>
    <title>A First JavaScript Program</title>
</head>

<body>
    <script language="JavaScript">
        document.writeln("<h1>Hello World!</h1>");
    </script>
</body>
</html>
```

The `<script>` tag indicates that what follows is an executable script. The `language="JavaScript"` attribute is not strictly necessary since JavaScript is the default value, but should be included as a matter of good style.

The `document.writeln` statement instructs the browser to display the string of characters enclosed in the quotation marks. If the string contains HTML tags, then these are interpreted by the browser; hence this example will cause the presented string to be displayed in the `h1` style.

The semicolon is the JavaScript statement terminator, and should appear at the end of each statement. Again, this is more a matter of good practice, since the JavaScript interpreters in most browsers will excuse a missing semicolon at the end of a line of code.

4.1.2   Variables and Simple Arithmetic

Consider Figure 4.2 that obtains two integer values from the user and calculates and presents their sum.

Note the form of comments used in this example. This is specifically for single line comments as everything from the comment marker // to the end of the line is ignored by the JavaScript interpreter. Another form of comments is available for multiple lines as follows:

```
/* This comment is
   spread over a
   number of lines */
```

JavaScript requires us to declare any variables used in advance (in reality some browsers do not require advance declaration, but it is a good idea to adhere to the convention). We can do this by using the `var` statement as described in this example. We can declare as many variables as we like with a single `var` as long as we separate them with commas. Variable names can be any combination of letters, digits and underscores as long as the name does not start with a digit.

Figure 4.2
I/O and Simple
Arithmetic

```html
<html>
<head>
    <title>I/O and Simple Arithmetic</title>
</head>

<body>
  <script language="JavaScript">
   // first the variable declarations
   var firstValue, secondValue;
   var firstNumber, secondNumber, sum;

   // then get the two values from the user
   firstValue=window.prompt("Enter first number", "0");
   secondValue=window.prompt("Enter second number", "0");

   // now convert values obtained from string to integer
   firstNumber=parseInt(firstValue);
   secondNumber=parseInt(secondValue);

   // and calculate the sum
   sum=firstNumber+secondNumber;

   // finally, output the addition expression
   document.writeln("<h1>" + firstNumber + "+" +
                   secondNumber + "=" + sum + "</h1>");
  </script>

</body>
</html>
```

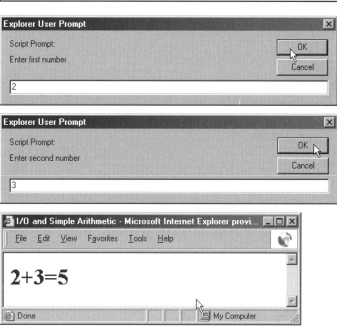

Input to JavaScript programs is facilitated by the `window.prompt` method that takes two parameters. These are a string prompt, and a default value to be returned if no input is provided by the user. If the default parameter is omitted, then the `null` value is returned.

The `window.prompt` method returns a string value, so as we want to add the user-supplied values together, we must first convert each to a numeric quantity. This is accomplished by the `parseInt()` function, after which we can simply add the integer values together by the arithmetic + (plus) operator.

Note particularly the second use of the + operator in the `document.writeln` statement. This time it is used to concatenate the various strings that make up the output parameter. Hence, for numeric values the + operator will calculate the sum of the operands, whereas for strings it concatenates them. This explains why we had to convert the strings to integers before we calculated their sum.

The set of basic arithmetic operators in JavaScript is shown in the following table.

Operation	*Symbol*	*Example*
Addition	+	2+3=5
Subtraction	-	5-3=2
Multiplication	*	3*2=6
Division	/	6/2=3
Modulus (Remainder)	%	9%5=4

4.2 JavaScript Control Structures

JavaScript makes available most (if not all) of the control structures one would expect to find in a modern high-level programming language. These can be divided into structures for selection and conditional execution, and structures for repetition and looping. In this section we also examine JavaScript assignment and comparison operators.

4.2.1 Conditional Statements

4.2.1.1 `if` and `if … else`

The **if** selection structure is used to choose between alternative paths in a program. For example, if a mark of 40% or greater is required to pass an exam, then an output statement might be formulated as follows

```
if (studentMark >= 40)
    document.writeln("You have passed");
```

Note the brackets around the condition —these are mandatory (as in C). The condition may contain any expression that can be resolved to one of the Boolean values **true** or **false**. Figure 4.3 provides the full set of relational and logical operators.

Figure 4.3
Relational and
Logical Operators

Relationship	Operator	Example
Equality operators		
Equal to	==	x == y
Not equal to	!=	x != y
Relational operators		
Greater than	>	x > y
Less than	<	x < y
Greater than or equal to	>=	x >= y
Less than or equal to	<=	x <= y
Logical operators		
And	&&	(x==1) && (y==2)
Or	||	(x < 2) || (y > 3)
Not	!	! (x > 10)

The `if … else` structure allows the programmer to specify an alternative action to be performed if the stated condition evaluates to false. For example, we may want to display a different message if the student's mark is below 40%, as follows.

99

```
if (studentMark >= 40)
   document.writeln("You have passed");
else
   document.writeln("You have failed");
```

If statements can also be nested to produce more complex conditions, as follows.

```
if (studentMark >= 70)
   document.writeln("First Class Mark");
else if (studentMark >= 40)
   document.writeln("You have passed");
else
   document.writeln("You have failed");
```

In these examples, we have only a single statement for each **if** or **else** clause. If we wish to expand this to include two or more statements in a block, then we must delimit the block with { and } as illustrated below.

```
if (studentMark >= 70) {
   document.writeln("First Class Mark<br>");
   document.writeln("Well done!");
}
else if (studentMark >= 40)
   document.writeln("You have passed");
else {
   document.writeln("You have failed<br>");
   document.writeln("Must try harder!");
}
```

4.2.1.2   switch

The **if...else** statement is sufficient for all occasions where we require some conditional program flow. Sometimes, however, we may meet the situation where we need to test a variable for each of the values it may take and perform different actions in each case. In such circumstances, the **switch** multiple-selection structure is a better option.

The form of the **switch** statement is as follows:

```
switch (testVariable) {

    case firstValue:    statements; break;
    case secondValue:   statements; break;
    case thirdValue:    statements; break;
    ... ...
    default: statements;
}
```

Note the **break** statement at the end of each **case** clause. This causes execution to skip to the statement immediately following the **switch**. If **break** is not used anywhere in a **switch** statement then each time a match occurs in the structure, every remaining **case** would be executed.

Figure 4.4 illustrates the use of the **switch** structure to display one of 5 HTML header levels determined by the input of the user.

Figure 4.4
The **switch**
Structure

```
<html>
<head>
    <title>Switch Selection Structure</title>
</head>

<body>
    <script language="JavaScript">
      var choice, theHeading;
      var validInput=true;
      choice=window.prompt("Select heading level (1-5)");

      switch (choice) {
         case "1": theHeading="<h1>Heading style 1</h1>";
                   break;
         case "2": theHeading="<h2>Heading style 2</h2>";
                   break;
         case "3": theHeading="<h3>Heading style 3</h3>";
                   break;
         case "4": theHeading="<h4>Heading style 4</h4>";
                   break;
         case "5": theHeading="<h5>Heading style 5</h5>";
                   break;
         default:  validInput=false;
      }
      if (validInput==true)
                   document.writeln(theHeading);
      else document.writeln("Invalid Choice");
    </script>
</body>
</html>
```

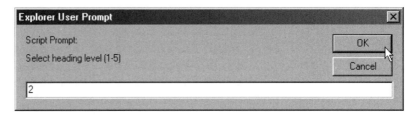

4.2.2   Loop Statements

4.2.2.1   `while`

The `while` construct provides a condition-controlled looping mechanism where the loop condition is tested before entering into the loop body. Figure 4.5 illustrates the `while` loop in a JavaScript program that presents all 6 header styles.

Figure 4.5
The `while` *Loop*
Structure

```
<script language="JavaScript">
  var counter=1;

  while (counter <= 6) {
    startTag="<h" + counter + ">";
    endTag="</h" + counter + ">";
    document.write(startTag + "Header level " +
                   counter + endTag);
    counter=counter+1;
  }

</script>
```

4.2.2.2 `for`

The **for** loop is used when we know in advance the number of times we want to loop to be executed. In the previous example, we know that we want to demonstrate six heading styles, so we could have written the code using a **for** loop as demonstrated in Figure 4.6.

Figure 4.6
*The **for** Loop*
Structure

```
<script language="JavaScript">

    for (var counter=1; counter<=6; counter++) {
        startTag="<h" + counter + ">";
        endTag="</h" + counter + ">";
        document.write(startTag + "Header level " +
                        counter + endTag);
    }

</script>
```

The **for** statement consists of three components, separated by semicolons, as identified below:

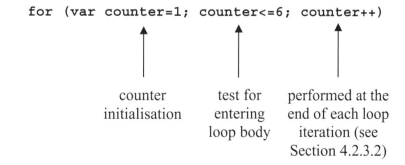

Note how the counter is both declared and initialised within the **for** statement. If we want to use a previously declared variable as our loop counter, then we can simply omit the **var**.

4.2.2.3   do ... while

The **do ... while** structure is similar to the **while** construct, except that the loop-continuation condition is tested at the *bottom* of the loop rather than at the top. Hence the body of a **do ... while** loop is always executed at least once, since the condition is only tested for the first time *after* the body has been executed. Figure 4.7 illustrates our header loop example written using the **do ... while** construct.

Figure 4.7
The do ... while
Loop Structure

```
<script language="JavaScript">
 var counter=1;
 do {
      startTag="<h" + counter + ">";
      endTag="</h" + counter + ">";
      document.write(startTag + "Header level " +
                          counter + endTag);
      counter=counter+1;
 } while (counter<=6)

</script>
```

4.2.2.4   break and continue

The **break** and **continue** statements alter the flow of control of the program. We have already met the **break** statement in the **switch** multiple-selection construct, where its purpose was to jump out of the **switch** structure after the desired statements had been executed. The **break** statement can also be used within any of the loop structures, where the effect is to jump immediately out of the current loop. Figure 4.8 illustrates the **break** statement used within a **for** loop to jump out of the loop after 5 iterations have been performed.

The **continue** statement also causes code to be skipped, but rather than jump out of the current loop structure, only the remaining statements in the current iteration are skipped —execution proceeds with the next iteration. Figure 4.8 also illustrates the **continue** statement within a **for** loop to prevent processing of iteration number 3.

Some developers feel that the use of **break** and **continue** within loop structures violates the principles of structured programming. It is certainly true that they result in code that is more difficult to read and follow, and so it is recommended that they should only be used sparingly and only when you are comfortable with their operation.

Figure 4.8
Using **break** *and*
continue

```
<script language="JavaScript">

    for (var counter=1; counter<=6; counter=counter+1) {
        if (counter==3) continue;
        startTag="<h" + counter + ">";
        endTag="</h" + counter + ">";
        document.write(startTag + "Header level " +
                        counter + endTag);
        if (counter==5) break;
    }

</script>
```

4.2.3 Assignment Operators and Data Types

4.2.3.1 Assignment

JavaScript provides several assignment operators for abbreviating assignment expressions. For example the statement

```
counter = counter + 3
```

can be abbreviated with the addition assignment operator += as

```
counter += 3
```

The `+=` operator adds the value of the expression on the right of the operator to the value of the variable on the left of the operator. The result is stored back in the variable. Assignment operators are also available for subtraction, multiplication, division and modulus.

Operator	Example	Equivalent to
+=	a += 3	a = a + 3
-=	b -= 3	b = b - 3
*=	c *= 3	c = c * 3
/=	d /= 3	d = d / 3
%=	e %= 3	e = e % 3

4.2.3.2   Increment and Decrement Operators

JavaScript also provides increment (`++`) and decrement (`--`) operators which cause the value of a variable to be adjusted by 1. They are available in both pre- and post-increment/decrement versions that allow us to combine the operators in other expressions, and determine whether we require the increment or decrement to occur before or after the variable is used in the expression. The increment and decrement operators are summarised below.

Operator	Example	Meaning
Preincrement (++)	++a	Increment **a** by 1, and then use the new value of **a** in the expression in which **a** resides
Postincrement (++)	a++	Use the current value of **a** in the expression in which it resides, then increment **a** by 1
Predecrement (--)	--b	Decrement **b** by 1, and then use the new value of **b** in the expression in which **b** resides
Postdecrement (--)	b--	Use the current value of **b** in the expression in which it resides, then decrement **b** by 1

4.2.3.3 Data Types in JavaScript

Unlike most programming languages, JavaScript does not require variables to be typed before they can be used. JavaScript is a *loosely-typed* language, and as such, a variable can contain a value of any type (*integer*, *float*, *character*, *string* or *Boolean*) at any time. In addition, JavaScript will frequently perform automatic conversion from one data type to another depending on how the variable is used. This can be seen by the following code fragment where a variable is created and used as an integer, and then output using the string concatenation operator.

```
var a, b, c;          // declare 3 variables
a="The value = ";     // a is assigned a string value
b=10;                 // b is assigned an integer value
c=a+b;                // c has the string "The value = 10"
```

4.3 Initialising and Using Arrays

An array is a group of variables that share the same name and are normally of the same type (although this is not required in JavaScript). The elements of an array are distinguished by their index, which is assigned with the first element having index 0, the second having index 1 and so on. Unlike arrays in many programming languages, JavaScript arrays are dynamic structures which can change size after they are created.

4.3.1 Declaring and Using Arrays

The declaration and initialisation of JavaScript arrays is illustrated by Figure 4.9 which presents four ways of declaring and initializing identical five-element arrays with the values of the elements set to 0, 1, 2, 3 and 4 respectively. Note that the first index position is 0 and the last index position is one less than the number of elements (hence for 5 elements the index positions run from 0 to 4). When we attempt to access an array element outside the bounds of the array (say, with the statement `a1[7] = 6;` then the JavaScript interpreter will automatically allocate more space (in this case `a1[5]`, `a1[6]` and `a1[7]`) so that the array will contain the appropriate number of elements.

Figure 4.9
Declaring and
Initialising Arrays

```
<script language="JavaScript">

var a1 = new Array(5);
var a2 = new Array();
var a3 = new Array(0, 1, 2, 3, 4);
var a4 = [0, 1, 2, 3, 4];

for (var x=0; x<a1.length; x++)
    a1[x] = x;

for (x=0; x<5; x++)
    a2[x] = x;

</script>
```

4.3.2   The `for` ... `in` Loop Structure

JavaScript provides a very useful control structure especially for traversing array elements. Consider Figure 4.10, which declares and prints out the contents of an array.

Figure 4.10
The ***for*** *...* ***in***
Loop Structure

```
<script language="JavaScript">

var a1 = new Array(2, 4, 6, 8, 10);

for (var x=0 in a1)
    document.writeln("Value at position " + x +
                     " is " + a1[x] + "<br>");

</script>
```

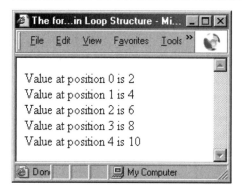

The **for ... in** structure is an abbreviated form of the **for** construct which automatically updates the loop counter and implements the termination condition to count across each element of the specified array. It is particularly useful in conjunction with dynamic arrays and the **arrayName.length** object since it means that the programmer does not need to maintain a variable that holds the number of elements in the array.

4.3.3 Multiple-dimension Arrays

Multiple-dimension arrays are specified by providing the information for each dimension in **[ ]** exactly as previously. Hence the statement

```
var a1[5][4]
```

declares an array of 5 rows and 4 columns. In order to access the data from (say) row 3 and column 1, the following notation is used:

```
a1[3][1]
```

A multiple-dimension array in which each row has a different number of columns can be described as an array of arrays, as (e.g.)

```
var b = new Array(2);
b[0] = new Array(5);
b[1] = new Array(2);
```

This would create the following two-dimensional structure, where the first row (**b[0]**) has 5 elements and the second row (**b[1]**) has 2 elements.

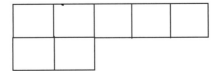

4.4   Functions in JavaScript

4.4.1   Defining Functions

Functions allow us to create programs that are easier to maintain and follow. A function is a self-contained piece of code that performs a well-defined task and has a correspondingly well-defined interface with the rest of the program.   Functions are defined in JavaScript by the keyword **function** as illustrated by Figure 4.11 below, which uses a function to return an example of an HTML header tag, where the header level required is presented in the function parameter.

Figure 4.11
Defining and Using
Functions

```
<script language="JavaScript">

for (var count=1; count<=6; count++)
    document.writeln (showHeader(count));

// definition for the function

function showHeader(thisLevel) {
    return "<h" + thisLevel + ">Header level " +
           thisLevel + "</h" + thisLevel + ">"
}

</script>
```

110

The mechanism for defining and using functions is very similar to that in other programming languages, but there are a few points worth noting.

1. The function need not be defined before it is used. As JavaScript is an interpreted language, the call **showHeader(count)** passes control to the function, wherever in the code it resides.

2. Function parameters are not declared with the **var** keyword. Use of **var** in this context will result in an error.

3. Any variables declared within the function body are local to that function and cannot be accessed from the main script body. In contrast, variables declared in the main script body are global —hence they can be accessed within functions.

4. Although the code in this example can reside in either the head or the body of the web page, it is more usual to define functions within the head, with the calling code placed at the appropriate point in the body.

4.4.2 Passing Parameters

Parameters to JavaScript functions are always passed by value. Hence, changes made to the values of parameters are not preserved when the function returns to the calling code. This organisation is illustrated by Figure 4.12.

The exception to parameter passing is arrays, which are always passed by reference (i.e. changes made to array elements inside functions are maintained after the function has been exited).

Figure 4.12
Passing parameters

```
<script language="JavaScript">

var x=1;
document.writeln("Before function: value is " +
                 x + "<br>");
add2(x);
document.writeln("After function: value is " +
                 x + "<br>");

// definition for the function

function add2(y) {
    y+=2;
    document.writeln("Inside function: value is " +
                     y + "<br>");
}

</script>
```

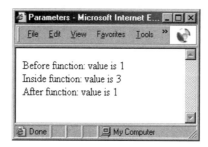

4.4.3 Recursion

A recursive function is one that calls itself in a controlled manner. JavaScript supports recursion in exactly the same way as any other function call, and we illustrate this through the example in Figure 4.13 which generates the 6 header types.

Figure 4.13
Using Recursion

```
<script language="JavaScript">
showHeader(1);

function showHeader(counter) {
    if (counter>6) return;
    else { document.write("<h" + counter +
                          ">Header level " + counter +
                          "</h" + counter + ">");
           showHeader(counter+1);
         }
}
</script>
```

Recursive functions require an exit condition as well as a recursive call. In this example, the exit condition is `counter>6`, which breaks the recursive cycle.

4.5   JavaScript Objects

We have already come across some of the predefined JavaScript objects —namely `document` and `window` (provided by the web browser) and `Math` and `Array` (native to the JavaScript language). Indeed, JavaScript is often referred to as an object-based programming language. This section presents three of the most useful JavaScript objects —`Math`, `String` and `Date` —and the operations that they make available.

4.5.1   The `Math` Object

The `Math` object provides methods that allow us to perform many common mathematical calculations. The methods presented in this section are used by quoting the name of the object (`Math` in this case) followed by a dot, the name of the method and a parenthesised list of arguments. For example to display the square root of 100 using the `sqrt` method, we state

```
document.write( Math.sqrt(100) );
```

The most commonly used methods in the `Math` object (although not an exhaustive list) are summarised in the following table.

Method	Description	Example
`abs(x)`	Absolute value of x	`Math.abs(-10) = 10`
`ceil(x)`	Rounds x to the smallest integer not less than x	`Math.ceil(9.2) = 10`
`floor(x)`	Rounds x to the largest integer not greater than x	`Math.floor(9.2) = 9`

113

`max(x, y)`	Largest of x and y	`Math.max(3, 5) = 5`
`min(x, y)`	Smallest of x and y	`Math.min(3, 5) = 3`
`pow(x, y)`	x raised to the power of y	`Math.pow(2, 3) = 8`
`random()`	Returns a random value in the range 0.0 —0.9999....	`Math.random() = 0.463`
`round(x)`	Rounds x to the nearest integer	`Math.round(9.2) = 9` `Math.round(9.7) = 10`
`sqrt(x)`	Square root of x	`Math.sqrt(16) = 4`

4.5.2 The `String` Object

A string is a series of characters treated as a single entity and is an instance of the object class `String`. String constants are written in JavaScript as a sequence of characters enclosed in either double or single quotation marks. `String`s can be compared using the relational operators `<`, `<=`, `>` and `>=` and the equality operators `==` and `!=`.

The most commonly used `String` methods are described by the following table. These are called by quoting the source string (i.e. that to which the operation is being performed) followed by a period, the name of the method and any parameters in parenthesis. For example, to return the substring *"Web"* from the source string *"Multimedia Web Programming"* we might have the following:

```
var str = "Multimedia Web Programming"
document.writeln( "the second word is " +
                  str.substr(11, 3) );
```

Method	Description
`charAt(index)`	Returns the character at the specified `index`
`indexOf(s,i)`	Searches for the first occurrence of `s` starting from position `i`
`join(s)`	Conbine an array of strings inserting `s` between each pair

`lastIndexOf(s,i)`	Searches for the **last** occurrence of **s** starting from position **i**
`split(string)`	Splits the source string into an array of substrings where the **string** argument specifies the delimiter
`substr(start,len)`	Returns a substring of **len** characters starting from position **start**
`toLowerCase()`	Converts the source string to lowercase
`toUpperCase()`	Converts the source string to uppercase

4.5.3   The `Date` Object

The `Date` object enables JavaScript applications to determine and manipulate the time and date at the browser. In order to obtain the current time and date in a variable **now**, we use the code

```
var now = new Date();
```

The component parts of the time and date can then be obtained by using methods in the form

```
var day = now.getDate();
var month = now.getMonth();
var hours = now.getHours();
var minutes = now.getMinutes();
```

We can also set the date and/or time by presenting parameters in a variety of formats as illustrated below

```
var myDate = new Date (June 23, 2005);
var myDate = new Date (June 23, 2005 14:07:23);
var myDate = new Date (05, 06, 23);
var myDate = new Date (05, 06, 23, 14, 07, 23);
```

The most commonly used `Date` methods are summarised in the following table.

Method	Description
getDate()	Returns the day of the month from 1-31.
getDay()	Returns the day in the range 0-6, where 0=Sunday, 1=Monday, and so on.
getMonth()	Returns the month in the range 0-11, where 0=January, 1=February, and so on.
getFullYear()	Returns the year in a 4-digit format (e.g. 2005).
getHours()	Returns the hours in the range 0-23.
getMinutes()	Returns the minutes in the range 0-59.
getSeconds()	Returns the seconds in the range 0-59.

4.6   Creating Animations with JavaScript

Previous chapters have introduced the use of CSS properties and their modification in response to user and browser events. It is possible to create complex effects by using JavaScript iteration and selection constructs to animate these properties over a period of time.

4.6.1   Programmed Animation

The simplest way to create JavaScript animation is to modify the `style` properties of an object inside one of the loop constructs. Figure 4.14 demonstrates this technique by animating the `left` and `top` properties of an image inside a `for` loop. The animation starts in response to the user clicking on the image.

The code in Figure 4.14 specifies that the ball object moves from position (10, 10) to position (110, 100) at a smooth rate by repeatedly incrementing the `left` and `top` style properties. This is a simple technique, which can be applied to any `style` property of any object, but it suffers from the disadvantage that the only way of controlling the rate of animation is to modify the amount by which the relevant property is modified on each iteration of the loop. If we wanted the object to speed up or slow down, then we would increase or decrease the amount by which the property is modified.

A more effective approach is to specify not only the amount by which the property is modified, but also the precise time at which modification takes place.

Figure 4.14
Simple Animation

```
<script language="JavaScript">
   var xPos=10, yPos=10;

   function moveObject() {
      for (var move=1; move<=100; move++) {
         theObject.style.left=xPos+move;
         theObject.style.top=yPos+move;
      }
   }
</script>

<img id="theObject" src="ball.gif"
    style="position:absolute; top:10; left:10"
    onclick="moveObject()">
```

4.6.2   Timed Animation

Time-driven animations can be controlled by adopting an interrupt-driven approach. By this method, we repeatedly specify the point in the future at which the next modification should take place.

This is enabled by the JavaScript function **setTimeout()**, which takes two parameters —a JavaScript function to be executed, and the number of milliseconds we want to wait before execution takes place. For example, the JavaScript statement

```
setTimeout ("doAnimation()", 1000)
```

117

would specify that we want the function **doAnimation()** to be executed exactly one second (1000 milliseconds) after execution of the **setTimeout()** function. Note that this does not pause execution of the script; rather, execution of subsequent statements continues in the normal way, and the specified function executes in parallel at the designated time.

Figure 4.15 illustrates the use of the **setTimeout()** function to control the animation of an image object from position (50, 0) to position (300, 0).

Figure 4.15

Interrupt-driven Animation

```
<html>
<head>
  <script language="JavaScript">
    var xSpeed=1;
    var xPos=0;

    function moveBall() {
      xPos+=xSpeed;
      ball.style.left=xPos;
      coords.innerText="Ball position: ("+xPos+", 50)";
      if (xPos<300) setTimeout("moveBall()", 10);
    }
  </script>
</head>

<body onload="moveBall()">
  <h2 id="coords">Ball position: (0, 50)</h2>
  <img id="ball" src="ball.gif"
      height="80" width="80"
      style="position:absolute; top:50; left:0">
</body>
</html>
```

The animation in Figure 4.15 is controlled by the function **moveBall()**, which adjusts the **left style** property of the image by the value of the variable **xSpeed** each time it is invoked. The last statement of the function schedules the next call of the function to happen in 10 milliseconds' time. Thus, for an **xSpeed** value of 1, the image moves from left to right at a rate of 1 pixel every 10 milliseconds, or 100 pixels per second. The conditional clause in the last statement ensures that the animation is halted when the **left** property reaches a value of 300. In addition, the function updates the **innerText** property of the **<h2>** element to report the current position of the image as the animation proceeds.

For applications such as that presented in Figure 4.15 where the rate of animation (time before the next interrupt-driven call to the animation function) is constant, it can be more convenient to set up the interrupt once so that it is automatically invoked at the periodic rate specified. This is supported by a method of the DOM **window** object, and is illustrated in Figure 4.16, which presents the ball image "bouncing" inside an enclosed area.

Figure 4.16
Bouncing Ball
Animation

```
<html>
<head>
   <script language="JavaScript">
      var xSpeed=10, ySpeed=5;
      var xPos=200, yPos=200;

      function start() {
         window.setInterval("moveBall()", 10);
      }

      function moveBall() {
         xPos=xPos+xSpeed; yPos=yPos+ySpeed;
         if (xPos>=400-80 || xPos<=0) xSpeed=-xSpeed;
         if (yPos>=400-80 || yPos<=0) ySpeed=-ySpeed;
         ball.style.top=xPos; ball.style.left=yPos;
      }
   </script>
</head>

<body onload="start()">
   <span style="position:absolute; top:0; left:0;
                width:400; height:400;
                background-color:yellow; border:solid">

      <img id="ball" src="ball.gif"
           height="80" width="80"
           style="position:absolute; top:200; left:200">
   </span>
</body>
</html>
```

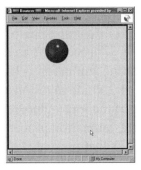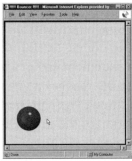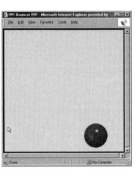

The **<body>** of Figure 4.16 presents an absolutely positioned **<span>** object with a solid border and a background colour, over which an image is positioned. When the page loads, the **onload** event handler invokes the function **start()** which sets up the interrupt-driven call to the animation function **moveBall()**.

Each time **moveBall()** is called (every 10 milliseconds), it updates the position of the image according to the values of the variables **xSpeed** and **ySpeed**. Before the change is committed to the **left** and **top** properties of the image, the conditional statements check that the new position does not exceed the boundaries of the **<span>**. When this is the case, then the **xSpeed** and/or **ySpeed** variables are inverted so that the ball changes direction —effecting the bounce off the edge of the arena.

Figure 4.17 further develops this application by implementing a game where the user is invited to click on the moving ball as many times as possible in a period of 10 seconds. The time remaining and number of hits so far are also reported to the right of the play area.

In this application we have three interrupt-driven functions to animate the ball (function **moveBall()**), control the timer display (**updateTimer()**) and terminate the game (**endgame()**). Note that we take advantage of the fact that the **window.setInterval()** method can return a value that acts as a handle to the interrupt driver, so that we can subsequently cancel the interrupt using **window.clearInterval()**. Hence, for the ball animation, the statement

```
animation=window.setInterval("moveBall()", 20)
```

determines that the function **moveBall()** is called every 20 milliseconds, and the statement

```
window.clearInterval(animation)
```

cancels the interrupt, so terminating the animation.

Figure 4.17
Interactive Game

```
<html>
<head>
  <script language="JavaScript">
    var animation,startTimer,stopTimer;
    var xspeed=5, yspeed=2;
    var xpos=200, ypos=200;
    var ballClickCount=0; var clock=10;
    var started=false;

    function start() {
      animation=window.setInterval("moveBall()", 20);
      startTimer=window.setInterval("updateTimer()",1000);
      stopTimer=window.setInterval("endGame()", 10*1000);
      started=true;
    }
    function endGame() {
      window.clearInterval(animation);
      window.clearInterval(startTimer);
      window.clearInterval(stopTimer);
      updateTimer();
      started=false;
    }
    function moveBall() {
      xpos=xpos+xspeed; ypos=ypos+yspeed;
      if (xpos>=400-80 || xpos<=0) xspeed*=-1;
      if (ypos>=400-80 || ypos<=0) yspeed*=-1;
      ball.style.top=xpos; ball.style.left=ypos;
    }
    function updateTimer() {
      time.innerText=--clock;
    }
    function updateBallCount() {
      score.innerText=++ballClickCount;
    }
  </script>
</head>

<body onload="start()">

<span style="position: absolute;
             top: 0; left: 0;
             width:400; height:400;
             background-color: yellow;
             border: solid">

  <img id="ball" src="ball.gif" height="80" width="80"
       style="position:absolute; top:200; left:200"
       onClick="if (started) updateBallCount()">
</span>
```

```
<h2 style="position:absolute; top:60; left:450;
        text-align:center">
    Time Remaining<br>
    <span id="time">10</span></h2>

<h2 style="position:absolute; top:200; left:450;
        text-align:center">
    Your score<br>
    <span id="score">0</span></h2>

</body>
</html>
```

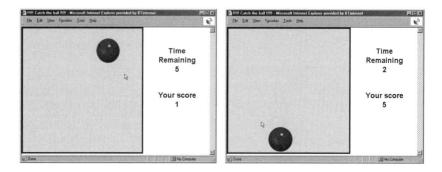

Figure 4.18 illustrates how JavaScript can be used to animate the parameters of DHTML filters as well as CSS **style** attributes. In this example, we have a **shadow** filter applied to an **<h1>** element where both the **direction** and **color** parameters are varied over time.

This example varies the **direction** parameter of the shadow every 500 milliseconds, demonstrating all the possible alternative values for the parameter (0, 45, 90, 135, 180, 225, 270, 315). On each complete rotation of the shadow (when the direction returns to 0), the **color** parameter is cycled to the next value in the **theColours** array.

Figure 4.18
Animated Filters

```
<head>
  <script language="JavaScript">
    var theDirection=0;
    var theColours=["red","blue","green","cyan",
                    "magenta","yellow"];
    var thisColour=0;

    function start() {
      window.setInterval("rotateShadow()", 500);
    }

    function rotateShadow() {
      theDirection+=45;
      text.filters("shadow").direction=theDirection;
      if (theDirection==360) {
        theDirection=0; rotateColour();
      }
    }

    function rotateColour() {
      thisColour++;
      if (thisColour==6) thisColour=0;
      text.filters("shadow").color=theColours[thisColour];
    }
  </script>
</head>

<body onload="start()">
  <h1 id="text"
      style="position:absolute; top:30; left:50;
             font-family:arial; font-size:24pt;
             color:black; padding:10px;
             filter:shadow(direction=0, color=red)">
    Demonstrating text shadows
  </h1>
</body>
```

123

SUMMARY

- JavaScript allows us to embed code in a web page that is interpreted by the browser on the client machine.
- JavaScript provides mechanisms for input/output and manipulation of variables.
- A set of language constructs for selection and iteration enable the implementation of complex algorithms.
- The type of JavaScript variables does not have to be specified. The JavaScript interpreter will converts variables from one type to another depending on the context in which they are used.
- JavaScript provides for programmer-defined functions. All parameters are passed by value except for arrays, which are passed by reference.
- JavaScript arrays provide flexible, multi-dimensional structures for data storage where any combination of data types can be stored in array elements.
- A selection of predefined objects provide a range of useful high- and low-level functions.
- Animated effects can be programmed by using JavaScript constructs to modify the CSS attributes of page elements.
- Timed animation is supported by an interrupt-driven mechanism that affords the programmer precise control over the rate of animation.

FURTHER INFORMATION

http://www.w3.org/DOM/
The World Wide Web Consortium DOM home page

http://www.w3schools.com/js/default.asp
W3Schools JavaScript tutorial

http://www.wdvl.com/Authoring/JavaScript/Tutorial/
JavaScript tutorial for programmers

http://www.webteacher.com/javascript/
JavaScript tutorial for non-programmers

http://www.javascript.com/
Collection of JavaScript resources and examples

http://www.webreference.com/dhtml/
JavaScript tutorial for non-programmers from WebReference.com

http://devedge.netscape.com/central/javascript/
The Netscape JavaScript Resource Centre

http://www.schrenk.com/js/
JavaScript Animation Tutorial

http://search.looksmart.com/p/browse/us1/us317831/us317881/us57
9926/us10209509/us10029804/us540309/
LookSmart Directory of JavaScript Animation tutorials

http://www.javascript-2.com/animation.html
Collection of JavaScript animation examples and resources

EXERCISES

1. Implement each of the code examples provided in the text. Try modifying various parameters in each example until you are comfortable with their operation.

2. Write a web page containing a script that asks the use to enter two numbers and then calculates and reports their sum, difference, product and quotient.

3. Write a web page containing a script that accepts from the user the radius of a circle and outputs HTML text that displays the circle's diameter, circumference and area. You should use the predefined object **Math.PI** for the value of π. Use the following formulae (r is the radius) —diameter = 2r, circumference = $2 \pi r$, area = $p \pi^2$.

4. Write a script that accepts a 3-digit integer from the user and displays each of the digits on a separate line of output.

5. Write a script that accepts 3 integers from the user and produces a web page with the following output:

   The largest value input was ...
   The smallest value input was ...
   The sum of values input was ...

6. Write a script that prompts the user for an integer in the range 1-12, advising the user of invalid input and requesting re-entry where appropriate. The script should then generate the multiplication table for that value (from 1x to 12x): e.g. for the value 6, the output should be:

   1 x 6 = 6
   2 x 6 = 12
   . . . . .
   12 x 6 = 72

7. Re-write the script from Exercise 1, so that the user also enters the limit of the multiplication table produced (in the range 1-20). Hence, for input of 6 and 4, the output should be

   1 x 6 = 6
   2 x 6 = 12
   3 x 6 = 18
   4 x 6 = 24

8. Write a script that accepts 5 integers from the user (in the range 0-20) and produces a histogram built using asterisks. For example the input 6, 12, 19, 8, 2 would produce the output:

   ```
   ******
   ************
   *******************
   ********
   **
   ```

Hint: you will need to generate the output using a fixed-width font such as Courier.

9. Write a script that reads in a series of 20 numbers from the user, and prints out the same list with duplicate numbers removed.

10. Write a script that accepts a string from the user and reports whether or not the string is a palindrome (spelt the same forwards as backwards). The palindrome check should ignore spaces and punctuation.

11. Develop a web page that illustrates a simple timeline animation as follows:

   a. Position 3 elements (paragraphs, images, headings, etc.) on the left hand side of the screen, one above the other.

   b. Have the elements move from left to right, started at 2 second intervals (where the top element moves first). Elements should stop when they arrive at a finishing line, where x=600.

   c. Vary the rate of movement for each element, so that all 3 elements arrive at the finishing line at the same time.

12. Modify the interactive game of Figure 4.17 so that the speed of the ball slowly increases as time elapses.

Using DirectAnimation Controls

CHAPTER OBJECTIVES

In this chapter, we address the following key questions.

- What is DirectAnimation?
- What is a DirectAnimation Control?
- How can we create two-dimensional graphics using the Structured Graphics Control?
- How can we apply transformations to Structured Graphics objects?
- Can we interact with Structured Graphics animations?
- How does the Path Control support timed and staged animations?
- What is the Sequencer Control and how is it used?
- How are sprites supported by the Sprite Control?
- How can we implement programmed animation using the DirectAnimation DAViewer Control?
- How does the DAViewerControl support mouse interaction?
- What facilities are available for creating complex three-dimensional animations?

5.1   Introduction to DirectAnimation

DirectAnimation is the component of Microsoft's DirectX API that provides graphics and animation support for web pages. The properties of DirectAnimation Controls are easily accessible through scripting, making possible a wide range of animated effects. Although Microsoft no longer officially supports DirectAnimation, it is supported by the latest versions of the OS and browser (Windows XP/Internet Explorer v6) and so remains a viable alternative for generating animated content on Microsoft browsers.

DirectAnimation is implemented as a collection of *ActiveX Controls*, which are built into the Microsoft OS and browser —each Control providing specific animation functionality. The following sections examine the application of each of the Controls in turn.

5.2   The Structured Graphics Control

The *Structured Graphics Control* is a web implementation of the DirectAnimation library —developed for use in interactive graphical applications. It allows us to create illustrations and diagrams by specifying them as a series of drawing commands.

5.2.1   Using the Control

Figure 5.1 presents a simple graphic element created with the Structured Graphics Control.

Figure 5.1
Using the
Structured Graphics
Control

```
<body>
  <object id="shapes"
     style="background-color:skyblue;
            height:200; width:400"
     classId="CLSID:369303C2-D7AC-11d0-89D5-00A0C90833E6">
     <param name="Line0001"
            value="SetLineColor(255,0,0)">
     <param name="Line0002"
            value="Polyline(2,0,-100,0,100">
     <param name="Line0003"
            value="Polyline(2,-200,0,200,0)">
  </object>
</body>
```

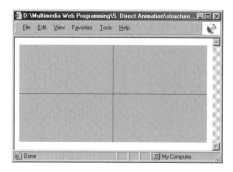

The graphic consists of a pair of line elements running horizontally and vertically across the centre of a coloured background.

The Structured Graphics control is embedded in the web page by an `<object>` tag with a specific `classId` attribute. Different `classId` values are used to identify the various DirectAnimation Controls available. The `style` properties of the object specify the size and colour of the drawing canvas. The Structured Graphics Control enables us to specify graphics by expressing them as a sequence of drawing instructions.

Each instruction is specified as a parameter (`<param>` tag) contained within the Structured Graphics `<object>`. Each `<param>` must be supplied with a `name` attribute in ascending order in the form `Line0001`, `Line0002` etc. If the `name` attribute is omitted, or the ascending sequence of `name` values is broken, then the drawing instructions will not be processed.

The `<object>` tag in Figure 5.1 specifies a Structured Graphics canvas 400 pixels wide and 200 pixels tall. Note that the point (0,0) is located in the *centre* of the canvas: hence the top left corner is coordinate position (-200, -100), while the bottom right corner is coordinate position (200, 100).

The value attribute of each `<param>` tag contains a drawing command. Here we specify the colour to be used when drawing lines by the `SetLineColor()` method, followed by a pair of `Polyline()` methods which specify the lines to be drawn. The `SetLineColor()` method takes three parameters, which specify the drawing colour in terms of red, green and blue —with each colour component specified in the range 0-255. Hence the command

```
SetLineColor(255, 0, 0)
```

sets the line colour to red.

The `Polyline()` method takes a varying number of parameters, depending on the number of points to be joined by the line. The first parameter specifies the number of points, while the remaining parameters specify each point as **x**, **y** coordinate values. Hence the command

```
Polyline(2, 0, -100, 0, 100)
```

draws a line between the points (0, -100) and (0, 100) —the vertical line in Figure 5.1.

5.2.2   Structured Graphics Methods

Figure 5.2 presents more of the drawing commands available in the Structured Graphics Control.

Figure 5.2
Structured Graphics
Methods

```
<body>
  <object id="shapes"
    style="background-color:skyblue;
            height:200; width:400"
    classId="CLSID:369303C2-D7AC-11d0-89D5-00A0C90833E6">
    <param name="Line0001"
          value="SetLineColor(255,0,0)">
    <param name="Line0002"
          value="SetLineStyle(1,5)">
    <param name="Line0003"
          value="Polyline(6,-200,-70,-50,-70,-50,-50,50,
                          -50,50,-70,200,-70)">
    <param name="Line0004"
          value="SetFillColor(255,255,255,255,255,0)">
    <param name="Line0005" value="SetFillStyle(9)">
    <param name="Line0006" value="SetLineStyle(2,1)">
    <param name="Line0007"
          value="RoundRect(-180,-30,360,110,30,30,0)">
    <param name="Line0008" value="SetLineStyle(0,0)">
    <param name="Line0009" value="SetFillColor(0,0,255)">
    <param name="Line0010" value="SetFillStyle(1)">
    <param name="Line0011"
          value="SetFont('Verdana',32,300,0,0,0)">
    <param name="Line0012"
          value="Text('Structured Graphics',-110,2,15)">
  </object>
</body>
```

131

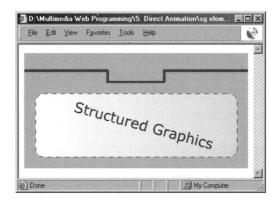

Figure 5.2 illustrates different styles for lines and fills, as well as presenting the rounded rectangle and text drawing objects.

The line style is set using the method **SetLineStyle()**, which takes two parameters: the type of line required, and the width of the line in pixels. Two line types are available, solid (1) and dashed (2); while a line style of 0 denotes that no line or border should be drawn. The effect of the line types can be seen in Figure 5.2 where the line object uses the solid style, the rounded rectangle has a dashed line border and the text element is drawn with no border.

The rounded rectangle and text elements also illustrate some of the potential for fill styles in Structured Graphics, where the former is filled with a gradient from left to right, while the latter is filled with a solid colour. The type of fill required is specified by the **SetFillStyle()** method, which takes a single parameter in the range 0-14 corresponding to one of a number of colour gradient and hatch styles.

The colour to be used when applying the selected fill style is specified by the **SetFillColor()** method. This takes either three or six parameters depending on the number of colours required by the fill style. Where the fill style requires a single colour (such as the solid fill used for the text), then the fill colour is specified as an RGB triplet. Where two colours are required (such as the gradient fill used in the rounded rectangle), then a pair of RGB triplets is required.

The rounded rectangle element is created by the **RoundRect()** method with parameters as follows:

```
RoundRect (x,y,height,width,rx,ry,rotation)
```

`x, y`	the coordinate position of the upper left corner
`height, width`	the dimensions in pixels of the element
`rx, ry`	the width and height of the rounded arc at each corner of the rectangle
`rotation`	the amount in degrees by which the element is rotated around its origin, in a clockwise direction

If we require a rectangle element with square corners, we can either set the `rx` and `ry` parameters to 0, or use the dedicated `Rect()` method which omits these parameters; hence

```
Rect (x,y,height,width,rotation)
```

Structured Graphics text elements are controlled by the methods `SetFont()`, which specifies the appearance of text elements, and `Text()`, which specifies the string to be displayed and its position on the canvas. The `SetFont()` method controls all aspects of text appearance as follows.

```
SetFont ('font',height,weight,italic,
                        underline,strikethrough)
```

where `'font'` is the name of the font to be used, `height` is expressed in pixels, and `weight` is in the range 100, 200, 300, …, 700. The parameters `italic`, `underline` and `strikethrough` are 1 if the effect is required, and 0 otherwise. The `Text()` method takes four parameters, detailing the string to be displayed, as well as an x, y coordinate position and rotation in degrees as before. Hence the drawing command

```
Text('Structured Graphics',-110,20,15)
```

specifies that the text object "Structured Graphics" is displayed at coordinate position (-110, 20) and is rotated 15 degrees in a clockwise direction.

Structured Graphics also provides methods to draw polygons, ovals, arcs and pie slices as illustrated by Figure 5.3. The `Polygon()` method takes the same parameters as `Polyline()` and generates an enclosed arbitrary shape. Methods `Arc()` and `Pie()` have a similar relationship to that of `Polyline()` and `Polygon()` in that `Arc()` produces a section of the circumference of an oval, while `Pie()` generates an enclosed shape by adding straight edges from each endpoint of the arc to the centre of the oval. `Arc()` and `Pie()` are expressed as

```
Arc (x,y,height,width,start,size,rotation)
```

where **x** and **y** specify the top left corner of the imaginary box that bounds the element, and **height** and **width** control the dimensions of that bounding box. Parameters **start** and **size** specify the portion of the oval used to generate the arc or pie slice, where **start** is the starting position in degrees and **size** specifies the size of the slice in degrees. Parameter **rotation** enables the element to be rotated as before.

Figure 5.3
More Methods

```
<body>
   <object id=shapes
      style="background-color:skyblue;
             height:200; width:400"
      classId="CLSID:369303C2-D7AC-11d0-89D5-00A0C90833E6">
      <param name="Line0001"
             value="SetLineColor(255,0,255)">
      <param name="Line0002" value="SetLineStyle(1,3)">
      <param name="Line0003" value="SetFillStyle(1)">
      <param name="Line0004"
             value="SetFillColor(255,255,0)">
      <param name="Line0005"
             value="Pie(-102,-48,100,100,345,60,0)">
      <param name="Line0006" value="SetFillStyle(7)">
      <param name="Line0007"
             value="Pie(-120,-50,110,110,45,300,0)">
      <param name="Line0008" value="SetFillStyle(8)">
      <param name="Line0009"
             value="Polygon(3,100,-70,50,30,150,-70)">
      <param name="Line0010" value="SetFillStyle(1)">
      <param name="Line0011" value="Oval(20,40,30,20,-45)">
      <param name="Line0012"
             value="Arc(-108,-60,120,120,345,60,0)">
   </object>
</body>
```

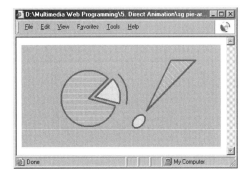

5.2.3 Animating Structured Graphics Objects

5.2.3.1 Translation

The Structured Graphics Control provides a number of methods that enable us to apply transformations to our drawings. Figure 5.4 illustrates how we can use the **translate()** method within a JavaScript function to provide animation of a graphical object.

Figure 5.4
Translation

```
<head>
<script language=JavaScript>
    var x=-150, direction=-1, rate=5;

    function start() {
        window.setInterval("translatePhoto()",100);
    }
    function translatePhoto() {
        if (x<=-150 || x>=50) direction*=-1;
        photo.translate(rate*direction,0,0);
        x+=rate*direction;
    }
</script>
</head>

<body onload="start()">
  <object id="photo"
     style="background-color:skyblue;
            height:200; width:400"
     classId="CLSID:369303C2-D7AC-11d0-89D5-00A0C90833E6">
    <param name="Line0001" value="SetLineStyle(0)">
    <param name="Line0002"
           value="SetTextureFill(0,0,'photo.gif',0)">
    <param name="Line0003"
           value="RoundRect(-150,-50,100,100,20,20,0)">
</object>
</body>
```

135

The **<body>** of Figure 5.4 implements a Structured Graphics object consisting of a rounded rectangle, to which an image has been applied using the **SetTextureFill()** method. The first two parameters of **SetTextureFill()** specify the position within the element where the image is to be applied, while the third parameter is the image to be used. The final parameter specifies whether to stretch the image to fill the available space (**0**), or to tile the image as many times as is necessary (**1**).

The **<head>** of the document contains JavaScript code to implement the animation. The function **start()** is called in response to the document's **onload** event and sets up an interrupt-driven call to the animation function **translatePhoto()**. This function maintains variables **rate** and **direction** to control the speed and direction of the animation. On each call, we check that the image has not reached the limit of the animation, changing direction as required; before calling the **translate()** function to move the image by a specified amount along the x-axis. The three parameters of the **translate()** function determine the distance to be moved in each of the x-, y- and z-axes.

5.2.3.2   Rotation

The **rotate()** function has a similar structure to **translate()**, and enables rotation of elements in three dimensions, as illustrated by Figure 5.5. Here, we apply a texture fill to an oval element, and implement an interrupt-driven function to animate its rotation.

Figure 5.5
Rotation

```
<head>
<script language=JavaScript>
    var count=1; angle=2;

    function start() {
        window.setInterval("spinPhoto()",50);
    }
    function spinPhoto() {
        switch (count) {
            case 1: photo.rotate(angle,0,0); break;
            case 2: photo.rotate(0,angle,0); break;
            case 3: photo.rotate(0,0,angle); break;
        }
        if (count++==4) count=1;
    }
</script>
</head>

<body onload="start()">
  <object id="photo"
      style="background-color:skyblue;
             height:200; width:400"
      classId="CLSID:369303C2-D7AC-11d0-89D5-00A0C90833E6">
      <param name="Line0001" value="SetLineStyle(0)">
      <param name="Line0002"
             value="SetTextureFill(0,0,'photo.gif',0)">
      <param name="Line0003"
             value="Oval(-63,-84,126,168,0)">
  </object>
</body>
```

The animation in Figure 5.5 is controlled by the function **spinPhoto()**, which rotates the image in turn around each of the x-, y- and z-axes, with the current axis determined by the value of the variable **count**. The **rotate()** method takes three parameters, corresponding to the angle of rotation in degrees for each of the axes.

5.2.3.3 Scaling

The final transformation method is **scale()**, which enables us to dynamically modify the size of a Structured Graphics object in each of the x-, y- and z-dimensions. Figure 5.6 presents an example where an object is made progressively bigger in x and then in y for three iterations, before being made progressively smaller again. As for **translate()** and **rotate()**, the **scale()** function takes three parameters which describe the scaling factor to be applied to each of the dimensions.

Figure 5.6
Scaling

```
<head>
<script language=JavaScript>
    var count=5; factor=1.3;

    function start() {
        window.setInterval("scalePhoto()",500);
    }
    function scalePhoto() {
        switch (count) {
            case 1: case 3: case 5: photo.scale(factor,1,1);
                                    break;
            case 2: case 4: case 6: photo.scale(1,factor,1);
                                    break;
        }
        if (count++==7) {
            count=1; factor=1/factor;
        }
    }
</script>
</head>

<body onload="start()">
  <object id="photo"
      style="background-color:skyblue;
             height:200; width:400"
      classId="CLSID:369303C2-D7AC-11d0-89D5-00A0C90833E6">
      <param name="Line0001" value="SetLineStyle(0)">
      <param name="Line0002"
             value="SetTextureFill(0,0,'photo.gif',0)">
      <param name="Line0003"
             value="Rect(-84,-63,168,126,0)">
  </object>
</body>
```

5.2.3.4 Interactive Structured Graphics

The examples in Figures 5.4, 5.5 and 5.6 demonstrated animation of Structured Graphics elements in response to an **onload** event. Once initiated, the animations in these examples run without any intervention from the user. It is possible to further extend the scope of our Structured Graphics animations by using some of the JavaScript animation techniques of the previous chapter.

Figure 5.7 extends the translation example from Figure 5.4 by adding a pair of button objects with which the user can increase or decrease the speed of the animation. When the user clicks on one of the buttons, the new function **changeSpeed()** is called with the amount by which the rate is to be changed passed in a parameter. A positive value will increase the rate of animation, while a negative value will slow down the movement. Any combination of DHTML events and HTML Form elements could be used to provide user control of Structured Graphics animations in this way.

Figure 5.7
Interactive
Structured Graphics
Animation

```
<head>
<script language=JavaScript>
   var x=-150, direction=-1, rate=5;

   function start() {
       window.setInterval("translatePhoto()",100);
   }
   function translatePhoto() {
       if (x<=-150 || x>=50) direction*=-1;
       photo.translate(rate*direction,0,0);
       x+=rate*direction;
   }
   function changeSpeed(change) {
       if (rate+change>0) rate+=change;
   }
</script>
</head>
```

139

```
<body onload="start()">
<object id=photo
    style="height:120; width:300;
          position:absolute; top:10; left:10"
    classId="CLSID:369303C2-D7AC-11d0-89D5-00A0C90833E6">
    <param name="Line0001" value="SetLineStyle(0)">
    <param name="Line0002"
          value="SetTextureFill(0,0,'photo.gif',0)">
    <param name="Line0003"
          value="RoundRect(-150,-50,100,100,20,20,0)">
</object>

<div style="position:absolute; top:150; left:10">
    <button onclick="changeSpeed(2)">Faster</button> 
    <button onclick="changeSpeed(-2)">Slower</button>
</div>
</body>
```

5.2.3.5 External Source Files

The Structured Graphics Control provides a simple way of constructing graphical objects that we can incorporate and manipulate in web pages. However, the requirement to consecutively number each drawing command in a `<param>` tag can make it frustrating when we want to insert or remove a command in the middle of a long sequence, as we will be forced to renumber all commands after that point. One way around this is to specify the drawing commands in a separate file, and then to include this file in the Structured Graphics object by specifying it as the `value` attribute to a `sourceURL <param>` tag.

Figure 5.8 illustrates this by demonstrating a pair of text files *'oval.dat'* and *'box.dat'*. The Structured Graphics Control contains no drawing commands in `<param>` tags, but rather the tag

```
<param name="sourceURL" value="box.dat">
```

specifying the contents of that file as the commands to be processed
for that object. In addition, we also specify a pair of event handlers

```
onmouseover="sourceURL='oval.dat'"
onmouseout="sourceURL='box.dat'"
```

which cause the set of drawing commands used to toggle as the
mouse is moved on and off the object.

Figure 5.8
External Source Files
and Mouse Events

```
<body>
  <object id="photo"
     style="height:120; width:120;
            position:absolute; top:10; left:10"
     classId="CLSID:369303C2-D7AC-11d0-89D5-00A0C90833E6
     onmouseover="sourceURL='oval.dat'"
     onmouseout="sourceURL='box.dat'">
     <param name="sourceURL" value="box.dat">
  </object>
</body>
```

External File
'oval.dat'

```
SetLineStyle(0)
SetTextureFill(0,0,'photo.gif',0)
Oval(-50,-50,100,100,0)
```

External File
'box.dat'

```
SetLineStyle(0)
SetTextureFill(0,0,'photo.gif',0)
RoundRect(-50,-50,100,100,20,20,0)
```

5.3   The Path Control

The *Path Control* is provided as a means to animate the position of other controls (such as Structured Graphics objects) or HTML elements along some predefined path. The control accepts a number of parameters that allow us to modify the properties of the animation.

5.3.1   Using the Path Control

Figure 5.9 illustrates the Path Control used to animate the position of an HTML heading element. The heading text traces the path of the oval specified in the **Target <param>** tag.

Figure 5.9
Using the Path Control

```
<body bgColor=purple text=white>
  <h1 id="myHeader" style="position:absolute">
      Path Control</h1>
  <object id="myPath"
     classId="CLSID:D7A7D7C3-D47F-11d0-89D3-00A0C90833E6">
     <param name="AutoStart" value="1">
     <param name="Repeat" value="-1">
     <param name="Duration" value="5">
     <param name="Bounce" value="0">
     <param name="Shape" value="Oval(20,20,150,50)">
     <param name="Target" value="myHeader">
  </object>
</body>
```

The parameters of the Path Control in Figure 5.9 are as follows:

AutoStart A value of **1** (or any non-zero value) determines that the control starts immediately the page has loaded. A zero value requires that the control be started explicitly through scripting.

Repeat	The number of times that the animation path is followed. A value of **–1** denotes that the animation will proceed indefinitely.
Duration	The time in seconds for a single iteration of the animation.
Bounce	Determines whether the animation terminates once the path has been followed (**0**), or reverses to its starting position (**1**).
Shape	A Structured Graphics element that describes the path of the animation.
Target	The element to which the control is applied.

Note also that to animate the position of the HTML element, its CSS attribute `position` must be set to `absolute`.

5.3.2   Multiple Path Controls

The Path Control is used to best effect when multiple controls are employed on a single page to cause elements to interact with each other in a single animation.

Figure 5.10
Multiple Path
Controls

```
<head>
 <style type="text/css">
    .countdown { position:absolute; font-family:verdana;
                 font-size:36pt; visibility:hidden }
 </style>

 <script language="JavaScript">
    var counter=0;
    function startTimer() {
      window.setInterval("startElement()",1000);
    }
    function startElement() {
      switch(++counter) {
        case 1: { three.style.visibility="visible";
                  threePath.Play(); break; }
        case 2: { two.style.visibility="visible";
                  twoPath.Play(); break; }
        case 3: { one.style.visibility="visible";
                  onePath.Play(); break; }
        case 4: { go.style.visibility="visible";
                  goPath.Play(); break; }
      }
    }
 </script>
</head>
```

```
<body onLoad="startTimer()">
 <span id="three" class="countdown" style="color:blue">
      3...</span>
 <span id="two" class="countdown" style="color:green">
      2...</span>
 <span id="one" class="countdown" style="color:purple">
      1...</span>
 <span id="go" class="countdown" style="color:red">
      Go!!!!!</span>

<object id="threePath"
    classId="CLSID:D7A7D7C3-D47F-11d0-89D3-00A0C90833E6">
    <param name="AutoStart" value="0">
    <param name="Repeat" value="1">
    <param name="Duration" value="2">
    <param name="Bounce" value="0">
    <param name="Shape"
          value="Polyline(2,350,10,50,100)">
    <param name="Target" value="three">
</object>

<object id="twoPath"
    classId="CLSID:D7A7D7C3-D47F-11d0-89D3-00A0C90833E6">
    <param name="AutoStart" value="0">
    <param name="Repeat" value="1">
    <param name="Duration" value="2">
    <param name="Bounce" value="0">
    <param name="Shape"
          value="Polyline(2,350,190,140,100)">
    <param name="Target" value="two">
</object>

<object id="onePath"
    classId="CLSID:D7A7D7C3-D47F-11d0-89D3-00A0C90833E6">
    <param name="AutoStart" value="0">
    <param name="Repeat" value="1">
    <param name="Duration" value="2">
    <param name="Bounce" value="0">
    <param name="Shape"
          value="Polyline(2,10,190,230,100)">
    <param name="Target" value="one">
</object>

<object id="goPath"
    classId="CLSID:D7A7D7C3-D47F-11d0-89D3-00A0C90833E6">
    <param name="AutoStart" value="0">
    <param name="Repeat" value="1">
    <param name="Duration" value="2">
    <param name="Bounce" value="0">
    <param name="Shape"
          value="Polyline(2,10,10,320,100)">
    <param name="Target" value="go">
</object>
</body>
```

In Figure 5.10 we animate four HTML `<span>` text elements to start from different locations on the canvas, and come together over a period of time to construct a single phrase. In contrast to the previous example, each element to be animated is initially hidden, and only made visible when it is started by invoking the control's `Play()` method. In addition, the `AutoStart` parameter of each Path Control is set to 0, and we explicitly start each animation through the JavaScript function `startElement()`, which starts one animation per second until all are under way. The path of each element is described by the `Polyline` supplied in each control's `Shape` parameter.

5.3.3   Using Time Markers

Time markers provide us with the facility to initiate events at any point in an object's path. These events can then be handled by JavaScript functions that affect some change to the appearance or location of some element. Figure 5.11 introduces the application of time markers to initiate a change in the `color` property of an HTML heading element as it proceeds along a path.

A time marker is created by a `<param>` tag of the form

```
<param name="AddTimeMarker1"
       value="2, mark1, 0">
```

The `name` attribute `AddTimeMarker` identifies the creating of a time marker. The suffix `1` is a sequence identifier, much in the same way as the `Line0001`, `Line0002` etc. identifiers in the Structured Graphics control. Hence subsequent time markers would have name attributes `AddTimeMarker2`, `AddTimeMarker3` and so on. The `value` attribute has three components, the first of which specifies the number of seconds after the path has started when the event is fired. The second value is an identifier by which the event will be known, and the final value determines whether we generate the event every time the path loops past this point (**0**), or only on the first iteration of the path (**1**). Hence in this case, we create an event to be fired 2 seconds after the start of the path, called "*mark1*", and which is generated each time the path loops.

Figure 5.11
Using Time Markers

```
<head>
   <script language="JavaScript"
           for="myPath" event="onmarker(marker)">
     if (marker=="mark1") header.style.color="yellow";
     else if (marker=="mark2") header.style.color="cyan";
     else if (marker=="mark3") header.style.color="white";
     else header.style.color="lightgreen";
   </script>
</head>

<body bgColor="darkred">
   <h2 id="header" style="position:absolute">
      Animating Text</h2>
   <object id="myPath"
       classId="CLSID:D7A7D7C3-D47F-11d0-89D3-00A0C90833E6">
      <param name="AutoStart" value="1">
      <param name="Repeat" value="-1">
      <param name="Duration" value="4">
      <param name="Bounce" value="1">
      <param name="Shape"
             value="Polyline(2,10,10,300,100)">
      <param name="Target" value="heading">
      <param name="AddTimeMarker1" value="0, mark1, 0">
      <param name="AddTimeMarker2" value="2, mark2, 0">
      <param name="AddTimeMarker3" value="4, mark3, 0">
      <param name="AddTimeMarker4" value="6, mark4, 0">
   </object>
</body>
```

In Figure 5.11, we generate four time markers for a Path Control animation. The events corresponding to the time markers are to be fired at the start of the path, and after 2, 4 and 6 seconds. Note that, although the Path **Duration** is only 4 seconds, the **Bounce** attribute is set to **1,** forcing the object to retrace its path, so that the actual duration of a single iteration is 8 seconds in total. The JavaScript code in the **<head>** defines an event handler for the **onmarker** event. When an event fires, the parameter passed to the event handler identifies the event that was raised. By testing this event against the **name** attributes of our time markers, we can then take the appropriate action.

5.4 The Sequencer Control

Previously, we have used the **window.setInterval()** function to control the timing of our animations. DirectAnimation also offers the *Sequencer Control*, which provides a simple mechanism for setting up events to take place at specified points in time.

Figure 5.12 revisits the animation of Figure 5.10 and uses a Sequencer Control to specify the time at which each of the animations is initiated.

Figure 5.12
The Sequencer
Control

```
<head>
  <style type="text/css">
    .textCount { position:absolute; font-family:verdana;
                 font-size:36pt; visibility:hidden }
  </style>

  <script language="JavaScript"
          for="sequencer" event="oninit">
    sequencer.Item("countdown").at(1,"show(three,
                                          threePath)");
    sequencer.Item("countdown").at(2,"show(two,
                                          twoPath)");
    sequencer.Item("countdown").at(3,"show(one,
                                          onePath)");
    sequencer.Item("countdown").at(4,"show(go,
                                          goPath)");
  </script>

  <script language="JavaScript">
    function startSequence() {
        sequencer.Item("countdown").Play(); }

    function show(object,path) {
        object.style.visibility="visible"; path.Play(); }
  </script>

</head>
```

147

```
<body onload="startSequence()">

<span id="three" class="textCount"
      style="color:blue">3...</span>
<span id="two" class="textCount"
      style="color:green">2...</span>
<span id="one" class="textCount"
      style="color:purple">1...</span>
<span id="go" class="textCount"
      style="color:red">Go!!!!!</span>

<object id="sequencer"
   classId="CLSID:B0A6BAE2-AAF0-11d0-A152-00A0C908DB96">
</object>

<object id="threePath"
   classId="CLSID:D7A7D7C3-D47F-11d0-89D3-00A0C90833E6">
   <param name="AutoStart" value="0">
   <param name="Repeat" value="1">
   <param name="Duration" value="2">
   <param name="Bounce" value="0">
   <param name="Shape"
         value="Polyline(2,350,10,50,100)">
   <param name="Target" value="three">
</object>

<object id="twoPath"
   classId="CLSID:D7A7D7C3-D47F-11d0-89D3-00A0C90833E6">
   <param name="AutoStart" value="0">
   <param name="Repeat" value="1">
   <param name="Duration" value="2">
   <param name="Bounce" value="0">
   <param name="Shape"
         value="Polyline(2,350,190,140,100)">
   <param name="Target" value="two">
</object>

<object id="onePath"
   classId="CLSID:D7A7D7C3-D47F-11d0-89D3-00A0C90833E6">
   <param name="AutoStart" value="0">
   <param name="Repeat" value="1">
   <param name="Duration" value="2">
   <param name="Bounce" value="0">
   <param name="Shape"
         value="Polyline(2,10,190,230,100)">
   <param name="Target" value="one">
</object>

<object id="goPath"
   classId="CLSID:D7A7D7C3-D47F-11d0-89D3-00A0C90833E6">
   <param name="AutoStart" value="0">
   <param name="Repeat" value="1">
   <param name="Duration" value="2">
   <param name="Bounce" value="0">
```

```
            <param name="Bounce" value="0">
            <param name="Shape"
                  value="Polyline(2,10,10,320,100)">
            <param name="Target" value="go">
      </object>
</body>
```

The **onload** event for the document in Figure 5.12 invokes the **startSequence()** function, which in turn initiates the **Play()** method for the those sequencer elements identified by the name "*countdown*". In response to the sequencer **oninit** event, the event handler specifies the time at which each of the four Path Controls should start. For example, the command

```
sequencer.Item("countdown").at(1,
                    "show(three, threePath)");
```

dictates that for the sequencer item identified as "*countdown*", the Path Control identified as "*threePath*" should be applied to the element identified as "*three*" after 1 second has elapsed.

5.5   The Sprite Control

5.5.1   Creating a Sprite

A sprite is a small graphic element that can be controlled independently from the image in which it appears. Sprites typically consist of a number of frames that are displayed in rotation to produce an animated effect. Figure 5.13 illustrates a sprite consisting of 7 frames, arranged in a 3 x 3 grid, which animate the display of the word "sprite". The blank cells in the grid create a pause between successive animations of the sprite.

Figure 5.13
Creating a Sprite

149

5.5.2 Using Sprites

DirectAnimation supports sprites by providing a control that enables us to treat an image as containing a number of frames that are animated at a specified rate. Figure 5.14 presents the image of Figure 5.13 as a Sprite Control.

Figure 5.14
Using Sprites

```
<body>
  <object id="sprite"
      classid="CLSID:FD179533-D86E-11d0-89D6-00A0C90833E6"
      style="width:200; height:100">
      <param name="Repeat" value="-1" />
      <param name="PlayRate" value="1" />
      <param name="NumFrames" value="7" />
      <param name="NumFramesAcross" value="3" />
      <param name="NumFramesDown" value="3" />
      <param name="SourceURL" value="spriteExample.jpg" />
      <param name="AutoStart" value="-1" />
  </object>
</body>
```

The parameters of the control determine how the image specified in `SourceURL` is divided into individual frames and displayed. The parameters `NumFrames`, `NumFramesAcross` and `NumFramesDown` describe how the image file *spriteExample.jpeg* (illustrated in Figure 5.13) contains 7 individual frames, organised within a 3 x 3 grid. The parameter `AutoStart` takes any non-zero value if the animation is to start immediately when the page loads, while the parameter `Repeat` specifies the number of times the animation is to be repeated, or –1 to make it loop continuously. The parameter `PlayRate` controls the rate at which the frames are displayed, where 1 is the default value and larger values cause the animation to speed up.

5.5.3   Interactive Sprites

The Sprite Control supports user interaction through the methods
Play(), **Stop()** and **Pause()**. Figure 5.15 demonstrates these by
having our sprite object react to mouse movement.

Figure 5.15
Interactive Sprites

```
<head>
   <script language="JavaScript">
      function goBackwards() {
         sprite.Stop();  sprite.PlayRate=-1;
         sprite.Play();
      }
      function goForwards() {
         sprite.Stop();  sprite.PlayRate=1;
         sprite.Play();
      }
      function pauseSprite() {
         sprite.Pause();
      }
   </script>
</head>

<body>
  <object id="sprite"
     classid="CLSID:FD179533-D86E-11d0-89D6-00A0C90833E6"
            style="width:200; height:100"
     onmouseover="goBackwards()"
     onmouseout="goForwards()" onclick="pauseSprite()">
   <param name="Repeat" value="-1" />
   <param name="PlayRate" value="1" />
   <param name="NumFrames" value="7" />
   <param name="NumFramesAcross" value="3" />
   <param name="NumFramesDown" value="3" />
   <param name="InitialFrame" value="1" />
   <param name="SourceURL" value="spriteExample.jpg" />
   <param name="AutoStart" value="-1" />
  </object>
</body>
```

If the mouse moves over the sprite, then the **PlayRate** attribute
is set to -1 to cause the frames to be displayed in reverse order.
When the mouse is moved off the sprite, then **PlayRate** is restored
to its original value. Note that the value of **PlayRate** can only be
changed when the animation is stopped.

5.6   Introduction to Scripted DirectAnimation

DirectAnimation provides a powerful library of functions and objects that are available through script to create complex interactive animations. The animations are presented within a **DAViewerControl**, specified within an **<object>** tag in the usual way.

5.6.1   Specifying a Drawing Area

Figure 5.16 demonstrates a simple graphic presented within a **DAViewerControl** object of dimension 300 x 150 pixels with a pale yellow background. The object is assigned a name (**DA** in this case) so that it can be referred to in the script.

The first line in the script creates a reference to the **PixelLibrary** of the **DAViewerControl**. The second line then calls the library's **NewDrawingSurface()** method to create a virtual canvas on which the presentation will be built. The following commands apply drawing primitives to the canvas before it is presented in the **DAViewerContol**.

Figure 5.16
Scripted
DirectAnimation

```
<body>
    <object id="DA"
        classid="CLSID:B6FFC24C-7E13-11D0-9B47-00C04FC2F51D"
        style="width:300; height:150;
                background-color:#ffff80">
    </object>

    <script language="JavaScript">
      m=DA.PixelLibrary;
      ds=m.NewDrawingSurface();

      ds.FillColor(m.Red);
      ds.BorderColor(m.Red);
      ds.Rect(-100,-50,130,80);
      ds.Oval(80,-30,50,100);

      ds.LineColor(m.Black);
      ds.LineWidth(2);
      ds.Line(-150,0,150,0);
      ds.Line(0,-150,0,150);

      DA.Image=ds.Image;
      DA.Start();
    </script>
</body>
```

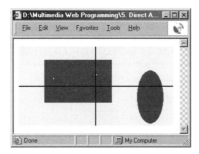

The first set of drawing commands set the fill and border colours, and generates the rectangle and the oval. Note how the drawing commands are methods of the virtual canvas created in the first line. Also note how the colour values are provided by the **PixelLibrary**, hence we refer to them as **m.Red** and so on.

The parameters of the **rect()** method are the *x*, *y* position of the top left corner of the rectangle, followed by the width and height. The **oval()** method takes four parameters corresponding to the *x*, *y* coordinate of the centre of the oval, followed by its horizontal and vertical radii.

The second set of drawing commands adds the two lines to the image. First we set the line colour and line width, followed by calls to the **line()** method with four parameters describing the *x*, *y* coordinates of each endpoint.

Finally, we transfer the image to the **DAViewerControl** by assigning the **Image** property of the Control to the corresponding property of the virtual canvas. Finally, we update the Control by invoking its **Start()** method.

5.6.2 Drawing Primitives

Figure 5.17 presents some of the other drawing primitives and transformations in DirectAnimation. After creating the virtual canvas, we set the colours and line styles used in the polygon object. Note how the library method **ColorRGB** can be used to create any colour value by expressing the red, green and blue parameters in the range **0-1**. The polygon is created by passing an array containing the coordinate data as a parameter.

Figure 5.17
Other Drawing
Operations

```
<body>
    <object id="DA"
        classid="CLSID:B6FFC24C-7E13-11D0-9B47-00C04FC2F51D"
        style="width:300; height:150;
                background-color:#ffff80">
    </object>

    <script language="JavaScript">
      m=DA.PixelLibrary; ds=m.NewDrawingSurface();
      ds.FillColor(m.ColorRGB(.5,.8,.9));
      ds.BorderColor(m.Black);
      ds.LineColor(m.Green); ds.LineWidth(3);
      ds.BorderWidth(2);

      points=new Array(20,10,130,50,100,60,40,50,40,70);
      ds.Polygon(points);

      ds.SaveGraphicsState();
      ds.Transform(m.Translate2(-150,-75));
      ds.Polyline(points);
      ds.RestoreGraphicsState();

      ds.RoundRect(20,-60,100,40,20,20);

      ds.PieDegrees(-125,25,0,135,50,50);

      ds.SaveGraphicsState();
      ds.Transform(m.Translate2(50,0));
      ds.ArcDegrees(-125,25,0,135,50,50);
      ds.RestoreGraphicsState();

      ds.LineColor(m.Black);  ds.LineWidth(2);
      ds.Line(-150,0,150,0);  ds.Line(0,-150,0,150);

      DA.Image=ds.Image; DA.Start();
    </script>
</body>
```

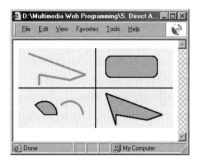

The same coordinate data is also used to draw the polyline object, by applying a translation. In order to implement the transformation, we save the current state of the canvas by invoking the `SaveGraphicsState()` method. We then translate the coordinate system of the canvas before drawing the polyline. A call to `RestoreGraphicsState()` removes the effect of the translation.

The rounded rectangle in the upper right quadrant is created by a call to the `RoundRect()` method with six parameters. The first two parameters specify the coordinates upper left corner of the element, while the next pair of parameters determines its width and height. The final pair of parameters describes the radius of the oval used to round the corners. The pie slice and arc elements provide another demonstration of translation. The parameters of both `PieDegrees()` and `ArcDegrees()` describe the x, y coordinates of the centre of the object, the start and finish angles of the slice (in degrees, measured anti-clockwise), and the width and height of the shape. Finally, we draw the axis lines and apply the image to the `DAViewerControl` as before.

5.6.3 Presenting Text

Figure 5.18 illustrates how we handle text elements in DirectAnimation. Here, we create three text strings and present them in different styles. The three elements are created separately and then merged onto the virtual canvas using the `Overlay()` method.

The first text element is created using the complex series of method calls

```
text1=m.StringImage("Text in DirectAnimation",
        m.DefaultFont.Family("Verdana").Size(32).
        Color(m.Blue));
```

This specifies both the text string and the style in a single statement. The string is created by the method `StringImage()` which requires two parameters —the string to be displayed and the style to be applied. Here, we specify the style by applying the `Family()`, `Size()` and `Color()` methods in series.

155

Figure 5.18

DirectAnimation Text

```
<object id="DA"
    classid="CLSID:B6FFC24C-7E13-11D0-9B47-00C04FC2F51D"
    style="width:600; height:150;
          background-color:#ffff80">
</object>

<script language="JavaScript">
  m=DA.PixelLibrary;  ds=m.NewDrawingSurface();

  text1=m.StringImage("Text in DirectAnimation",
          m.DefaultFont.Family("Verdana").Size(32).
          Color(m.Blue));
  text1=text1.Transform(m.Translate2(-80,-35));

  fs=m.Font("Arial",18,m.Red);
  text2=m.StringImage("Using a defined font style", fs);

  text3=m.StringImage("Modifying a previous style",
          fs.Bold().Italic());
  text3=text3.Transform(m.translate2(100,50));

  DA.Image=m.Overlay(text1, m.Overlay(text2,
                           m.Overlay(text3, ds.Image)));
  DA.Start()
</script>
```

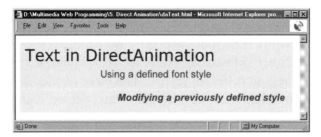

For the second text element, we demonstrate how to separate the specification of the style from the string. This is useful if we want to create a style to be applied to a number of string elements. The style is created by the **Font()** method, which takes the style properties (font name, point size and colour) as parameters. The style created can then be used as the second parameter to the **StringImage()** method.

The final text element illustrates how we can take a previously defined style and modify it in the **StringImage()** method by invoking the **Bold()** and **Italic()** methods. Each text string is created as a separate graphical element, which is translated into position. We then use a series of embedded **Overlay()** methods to compose the final image.

5.6.4 Mouse Interaction

DirectAnimation provides a set of program control methods that can be used in conjunction with mouse events to produce interactive animated presentations. Figure 5.19 presents an example which implements a red oval element that changes into a green rounded rectangle when the left mouse button is clicked on the element. If the right mouse button is clicked over the green rectangle, then it reverts back to the red oval.

Figure 5.19
Mouse Events

```
<object id="DA"
    classid="CLSID:B6FFC24C-7E13-11D0-9B47-00C04FC2F51D"
    style="width:300; height:150;
           background-color:#ffff80">
</object>

<script language="JavaScript">
    m=DA.PixelLibrary;

    ds1=m.NewDrawingSurface();
    ds1.FillColor(m.Red); ds1.BorderColor(m.Red);
    ds1.Oval(-50,-50,100,100);

    ds2=m.NewDrawingSurface();
    ds2.FillColor(m.Green); ds2.BorderColor(m.Green);
    ds2.RoundRect(-50,-50,100,100,30,30);

    final=new ActiveXObject("DirectAnimation.DAImage");
    final.Init(m.Until(ds1.Image,m.leftButtonDown,
            m.Until(ds2.Image,m.rightButtonDown,final)));
    DA.Image=final;
    DA.Start()
</script>
```

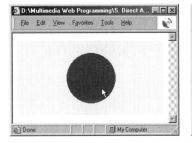 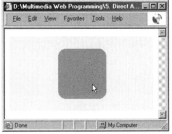

157

Each of the graphical elements is created on a separate virtual canvas, each created as usual by a call to **NewDrawingSurface()**. We then create a new **DAImage** object (**final**) to display the result of event processing. The interaction is implemented by a pair of nested **Until()** methods, which takes three parameters. The first parameter is the virtual canvas to be displayed prior to the named event, while the second parameter is the event to be handled. Finally, the third parameter is the virtual canvas to be displayed after the event is detected. Here, we state that the canvas **ds1** is presented until the left mouse button event is detected. After the mouse event, the canvas **ds2** is presented until the right mouse button event is presented, at which point the first condition is recursively invoked.

5.6.5   Animated Transformations

Figure 5.20 presents three graphical elements to which animated transformations have been applied. We have a blue box element rotated in three dimensions, a green oval element animated along a path, and a red oval element that grows and shrinks. All animations will repeat forever.

The animations are specified by the **Interpolate()** method, which takes three parameters —the endpoints of the interpolation, and the duration of the interpolation in seconds. Hence the code

```
m.Interpolate(10, 200, 3)
```

generates an ascending sequence of values from 10 to 200 over a 3-second period.

The animations are controlled by the functions **Scale2Anim()**, **Translate2Anim()** and **Rotate3RateDegrees()**. The first of these is applied to the red oval element, and interpolates the scaling of the radius between 20% (**0.2**) and 120% (**1.2**) of the original size. The two-dimensional translation is applied to the green oval element and causes it to move along a horizontal path. Finally, a three-dimensional rotation is applied to the blue rounded rectangle.

Figure 5.20
Animated
Transformations

```
<object id="DA"
   classid="CLSID:B6FFC24C-7E13-11D0-9B47-00C04FC2F51D"
   style="width:300; height:150;
          background-color:#ffff80">
</object>

<script language="JavaScript">
   m=DA.PixelLibrary;

   redOval=m.Oval(80,80).Fill(m.DefaultLineStyle,
                               m.SolidColorImage(m.Red));
   redOval=redOval.Transform(m.Translate2(40,-20));

   greenOval=m.Oval(30,30).Fill(m.DefaultLineStyle,
                                m.SolidColorImage(m.Green));
   greenOval=greenOval.Transform(m.Translate2(-120,50));

   blueBox=m.RoundRect(80,50,20,10).Fill(
          m.DefaultLineStyle, m.SolidColorImage(m.Blue));
   blueBox=blueBox.Transform(m.Translate2(-90,-30));

   scaleRate=m.Sequence(m.Interpolate(0.2,1.2,1.5),
              m.Interpolate(1.2,0.2,.5)).RepeatForever();
   redOval=redOval.Transform(m.Scale2Anim(scaleRate,
                                          scaleRate));

   moveXRate=m.Sequence(m.Interpolate(0,250,2),
               m.Interpolate(250,0,2)).RepeatForever();
   greenOval=greenOval.Transform(m.Translate2Anim(
                          moveXRate, m.DANumber(0)));

   boxTrans1=m.Translate2(-90,-30);
   rotFactor=m.Rotate3RateDegrees(m.Vector3(1,1,1),
                              60).ParallelTransform2();
   boxTrans2=m.Translate2(90,30);
   boxFinalTrans=m.Compose2(m.Compose2(
                    boxTrans1,rotFactor),boxTrans2);
   blueBox=blueBox.Transform(boxFinalTrans);

   DA.Image=m.Overlay(redOval,
                      m.Overlay(greenOval, blueBox));
   DA.Start();
</script>
```

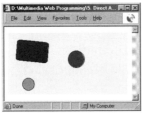 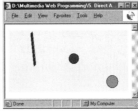 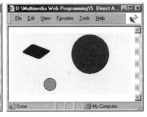

SUMMARY

- *DirectAnimation* is a Microsoft technology that supports graphical and animated content in web pages.
- The *Structured Graphics Control* provides a simple way of creating two-dimensional drawings from a range of graphics primitives.
- Structured Graphics drawings can be animated, and can be made to react to a selection of mouse events.
- The *Path Control* enables us to animate the location of any HTML content on the web page.
- The *Sequencer Control* supports complex animated sequences in which different elements are started at different times.
- The *Sprite Control* supports sprite-based animations.
- DirectAnimation provides a range of scriptable methods and objects that support the generation of complex programmed animation.

FURTHER INFORMATION

http://www.microsoft.com/mind/1097/directanim.asp
Adding Theatrical Effects to everyday web pages using DirectAnimation

http://www.cabinc.net/WTDirectAnimation/default.htm
Collection of DirectAnimation samples

http://www.newarchitectmag.com/documents/s=6092/new10136377 36/online.htm
Animating your web pages with DirectAnimation

http://www.pcprogramming.com/DAnim/DAnim.htm
Complex DirectAnimation samples

http://www.designerindex.com/dhtml/directx/
An animated spinning world created in scripted DirectAnimation

http://c2.com/cgi/wiki?DirectAnimation
An overview of DirectAnimation technologies

http://shuster.host.sk/javascript/samples/axrotateimage/
axrotateimage.html
Simple example – Rotating GIFs and JPEGs with DirectAnimation

http://www.templatemania.com/examples/Rotate/index.cfm
*Example – using the Sequencer Control to rotate a Structured
Graphics object*

http://msdn.microsoft.com/archive/default.asp?url=/archive/
en-us/dnardxgen/html/msdn_dx5media.asp
*DirectX Media: Multimedia Services for Microsoft Internet Explorer
and Microsoft Windows*

EXERCISES

1. Implement each of the code examples provided in the text. Try modifying various parameters in each example until you are comfortable with their operation.

2. Use the Structured Graphics Control to create a drawing of some everyday object (e.g. house, car, self-portrait!) from the basic drawing primitives. Use a range of colours and fills in your drawing.

3. Use the Structured Graphics Control to place an image on the screen, which is simultaneously rotated, scaled and translated as in Figures 5.4, 5.5 and 5.6. Add a button object which when pressed once stops the rotation transformation, and when pressed again restarts it. Add similar buttons for scaling and translation.

4. Modify Figure 5.9 so that the words "Path" and "Control" are animated along separate paths for a period of 3 seconds before making up the phrase "Path Control" in the middle of the display area.

5. Revisit Exercise 4, above, but use a Sequencer Control to start the animation of the word "Control" one second after the animation of the word "Path".

6. Use any drawing package to create a sprite that consists of a simple stick figure walking. Display this sprite on a web page using the Sprite Control.

7. Revisit your drawing from Exercise 2, above, and generate the same image using scripted DirectAnimation.

8. Use scripted DirectAnimation to create a welcome screen for a web site. The screen should consist of the word "W E L C O M E", where each letter is animated separately. Use a variety of paths, transformations and text styles to create the most appealing effect you can.

Scalable Vector Graphics

CHAPTER OBJECTIVES

In this chapter, we address the following key questions.

- What is Scalable Vector Graphics?
- How do we define and view SVG drawings?
- What are the basic graphic elements of SVG?
- How do we add text to SVG drawings?
- Can we group SVG elements and treat the groups as single objects?
- How can we make use of advanced fills and patterns?
- Can we set up fill and pattern styles and apply them to multiple objects?
- What effects can we achieve with filters and lighting models?
- How do we create event-driven SVG applications?
- How can we animate our SVG drawings?

6.1   Introduction to SVG and XML

SVG (Scalable Vector Graphics) is a notation for describing two-dimensional graphics in XML, for embedding into web pages. SVG allows for three types of graphic objects: vector graphic shapes (e.g. paths consisting of straight lines and curves), images and text. Transformations, filters and other effects can also modify objects. SVG drawings can be interactive and dynamic, with animations defined and triggered either declaratively (i.e. by embedding SVG animation elements in the SVG content) or via scripting.

6.1.1   XML – e<u>X</u>tensible <u>M</u>ark-up <u>L</u>anguage

The SVG notation is defined as an XML application. Although a detailed study of XML is beyond the scope of this text, we can easily pick up the structure of XML syntax by remembering the three primary rules of XML:

1. All attribute values must be enclosed in inverted commas. For example `color="blue"`.

2. All elements must have corresponding opening and closing tags. For example, the HTML tags `<p>` and `</p>`. Where a closing tag does not exist, such as `<img>` or `<br>`, then the tag must be specified with a trailing slash character, as `<br />` or `<img src="myImage.gif" />`

3. All tags must be written in lower case. XML (unlike HTML) is case-sensitive.

6.1.2   Creating an SVG Document

Figure 6.1 illustrates a first document in SVG.

Figure 6.1
SVG Document

```
<?xml version="1.0"?>
<!DOCTYPE svg PUBLIC "-//W3C//DTD SVG 20010904//EN"
"http://www.w3.org/TR/2001/REC-SVG-
20010904/DTD/svg10.dtd">

<svg>

  <!-- Draw a pair of squares -->

  <rect x="20" y="20" width="100" height="100"
       style="fill:yellow;  stroke:navy;  stroke-width:2"
/>

  <rect x="80" y="80" width="100" height="100"
       style="fill:green; stroke:red; stroke-width:5" />
```

The initial lines of this example define the contents as an SVG/XML document, and need not be changed from one document to another.

The **<svg>** object contains all of the code defining the graphical object. It is a requirement of XML that documents contain one *root element*, which contains all others. The **<svg>** tag fulfils this role.

The elements define a pair of square objects to be drawn on the canvas. These are generated by the **<rect />** element, with attributes **x** and **y** (the top left corner of the box), **width** and **height** (the size of the box), and **style** (which enables a range of presentation properties to be set).

Note that the "painters' algorithm" is used to resolve overlapping objects. By this technique, the elements are drawn in the order in which they appear in the SVG code, so that objects drawn later (in this case, the darker, green box) will be represented on top of objects drawn earlier (the lighter, yellow box).

Figure 6.2
SVG Output

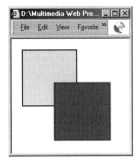

6.1.3 Viewing SVG

SVG images can be viewed either as standalone documents, saved with a **.svg** extension and loaded into a web browser, or as an embedded object within a web page. In the latter case, the **<object>** tag is used to embed the image, as illustrated in Figure 6.3, which embeds the code from Figure 6.1 (saved as "firstSVG.svg") into an HTML document.

In either case, the browser must have an *SVG viewer* installed. Such a viewer will soon be automatically included with all new browser releases, but for now a plug-in can be downloaded and installed from Adobe (http://www.adobe.com) if required.

Figure 6.3
Embedded SVG

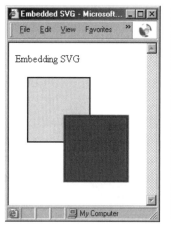

```
<html>

<head>
    <title>Embedded SVG</title>
</head>

<body>Embedding SVG<br>
    <object type="image/svg-xml"
        width=100 height=100
        data="firstSVG.svg">
    </object>
</body>

</html>
```

6.1.4 SVG Coordinate Systems

The **<svg>** element is much more powerful (and complex!) than presented so far. SVG elements are painted onto a canvas, which is potentially infinite in size. By default, the visible portion of the canvas is presented in an area defined by the dimensions of the browser, but this can be controlled by setting the **width** and **height** attributes of the **<svg>** element. For example the **<svg>** tag

```
<svg width="10cm" height="6cm">
```

specifies that the SVG elements will be presented in the browser within a rectangular area of width 10cm and height 6cm.

In addition, we can specify the portion of the infinite canvas to be presented by setting the **viewBox** attribute. For example, the `<svg>` tag

```
<svg width="10cm" height="6cm"
     viewBox="0 0 1000 600">
```

specifies that the visible portion of the canvas is described by the rectangle with upper-left coordinate position (0,0) and lower-right coordinate position (1000, 600). The mapping of **viewbox** coordinates to display area determines the scale at which the SVG elements are drawn.

One of the most useful features of the `<svg>` element is the ability to define graphic objects with their own coordinate system, which can then be reused by nesting including them within a parent `<svg>` element.

Figure 6.4 illustrates this by defining the overlapping squares graphic as a separate `<svg>` element that is then included within an SVG document. It is worth carefully studying the pair of `<svg>` tags used in this example.

The first `<svg>` tag in Figure 6.4

```
<svg height="8cm" width="8cm"
     viewBox="0 0 800 800">
```

specifies that the image is to be created on a canvas of 8cm by 8cm, with a coordinate range from (0,0) in the top left corner to (800, 800) in the bottom right corner. The location of components of the image (for example the first `<rect>` tag) is relative to this coordinate system.

The second `<svg>` tag

```
<svg x="400" y="400"
     width="300" height="300"
     viewBox="0 0 200 200">
```

Figure 6.4
Nested SVG

```
<?xml version="1.0"?>
<!DOCTYPE svg PUBLIC "-//W3C//DTD SVG 20010904//EN"
"http://www.w3.org/TR/2001/REC-SVG-
20010904/DTD/svg10.dtd">

<svg height="8cm" width="8cm" viewBox="0 0 800 800">

  <rect x="10" y="10" width="780" height="50"
        style="fill: blue" />

  <svg x="400" y="400" width="300" height="300"
      viewBox="0 0 200 200">

    <rect x="0" y="0" width="100%" height="100%"
          style="fill: yellow" />
    <rect x="20" y="20" width="100" height="100"
          style="fill: yellow; stroke: navy;
          stroke-width: 2" />
    <rect x="80" y="80" width="100" height="100"
          style="fill: green; stroke: red;
          stroke-width: 5" />
  </svg>

</svg>
```

identifies an area on the canvas bounded by the region (400, 400) to (700, 700) within which the overlapping squares logo will be created. In addition, the **viewBox** attribute specifies that this area is to have a coordinate range from (0, 0) in the top left corner to (200, 200) in the bottom right corner. The component parts of the logo (the three **<rect>** tags within the second **<svg>** element) are defined relative to this coordinate system. The effect of this code is shown in Figure 6.5.

Figure 6.5
Nested SVG

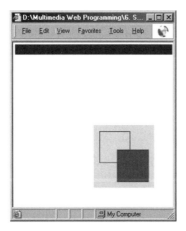

168

We can also use this example to illustrate how SVG images are dynamically scaled according to the characteristics of the canvas on which they are to be displayed. Figure 6.6 illustrates the effect of modifying the second `<svg>` tag to

```
<svg x="400" y="400"
     width="200" height="200"
     viewBox="0 0 200 200">
```

Figure 6.6
Scaled to Smaller
Area

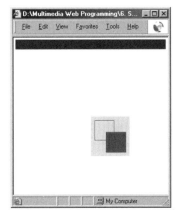

while Figure 6.7 shows the result of modifying the tag to

```
<svg x="400" y="400"
     width="400" height="400"
     viewBox="0 0 200 200">
```

Figure 6.7
Scaled to Larger
Area

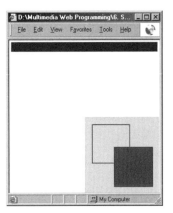

Note that we are not changing the coordinate system of the inner `<svg>` tag, but only the dimensions of the area in which the contents of the `<svg>` tag are to be rendered.

6.2 Basic Shapes

SVG supports the following basic shapes: `rect` (rectangle), `circle`, `ellipse`, `line`, `polyline`, `polygon` and `path`. The following sections illustrate an example of each, and identify the meaning of each of the parameters.

6.2.1 The `rect` Element

The `rect` element causes a rectangle to be drawn on the canvas. The size and location and physical appearance of the rectangle are specified by a collection of attributes such as those presented in the following sample tag.

```
<rect x="10" y="10" length="100" height="50"
      rx="15" ry="15"
      style="fill: blue;
             fill-opacity: 0.75;
             stroke: yellow;
             stroke-width: 3;
             stroke-opacity: 1" />
```

The `x` and `y` attributes specify the upper left corner of the rectangle, while the `length` and `height` attributes control the size of the object. The `rx` and `ry` values describe the x- and y-axis radii of the ellipse used to round the corners of the rectangle. Where these values are not provided (or are set to zero), then square corners are produced.

The `style` attribute is used to specify the CSS properties of the element. Here, the following properties are set.

fill

Specifies the colour to be used for the interior of the element. Colour values can be expressed in one of three ways. This example uses one of the named colours supported by CSS, with the syntax `fill:blue`. The colour could alternatively be specified as `fill:rgb(0,0,255)` where the colour is expressed in terms of its red, green and blue primary components with each component expressed in the range 0-255. Finally, the colour can be specified as a 6-digit hexadecimal quantity as `fill:#0000ff`.

`fill-opacity`
Defines the opacity of the interior of the element. Opacity values are expressed in the range **0** (totally transparent) to **1** (totally opaque).

`stroke`
Specifies the colour of the outline of the element. Colours can be expressed in any of the methods already identified.

`stroke-width`
Specifies the width of the outline of the element. The outline of an element is centred on the element's boundary; hence the stroke has the effect of increasing the width of the element by half of the stated stroke width. For example, if a rectangle of width 100 pixels is bounded by a stroke of width 5 pixels, then the width onscreen of the rectangle will be 105 pixels, with an overlap of 2.5 pixels on one side of the rectangle and an overlap of 2.5 pixels on the other side.

`stroke-opacity`
Defines the opacity of the boundary of the element, as previously described for fill-opacity.

Figure 6.8 illustrates a pair of overlapping `rect` elements with a variety of colours, opacity values and corner styles.

Figure 6.8
Overlapping SVG Elements

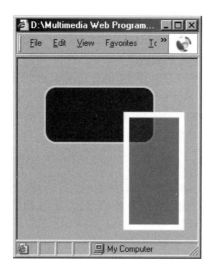

6.2.2   The `circle` Element

A `circle` element is described by its radius (attribute `r`) and the coordinates of its centre point (attributes `cx` and `cy`). In addition, a `style` attribute enables the specification of a range of CSS presentation properties.

Figure 6.9 illustrates a collection of overlapping circles with varying colours and opacities.

Figure 6.9
Overlapping Circle Elements

```
<?xml version="1.0"?>
<!DOCTYPE svg PUBLIC "-//W3C//DTD SVG 20010904//EN"
"http://www.w3.org/TR/2001/REC-SVG-
20010904/DTD/svg10.dtd">

<svg height="8cm" width="8cm" viewBox="0 0 400 400">

  <circle cx="100" cy="100" r="80"
          style="fill:rgb(255, 127, 127); fill-opacity: 1;
                 stroke: yellow; stroke-width: 3;
                 stroke-opacity:1" />

  <circle cx="100" cy="100" r="30"
          style="fill: red; fill-opacity: 0.5;
                 stroke: yellow; stroke-width: 3;
                 stroke-opacity:1" />

  <circle cx="200" cy="200" r="80"
          style="fill: blue; fill-opacity: 0.5" />

</svg>
```

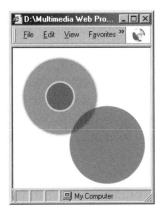

6.2.3 The `ellipse` Element

An ellipse is essentially a circle where the radius values in the x- and y-directions are different. In SVG, we therefore have **rx** and **ry** attributes to specify the x and y radii as

```
<ellipse cx="600" cy="200" rx="100" ry="50"
        style="fill: green stroke: black;
                stroke-width=: 10" />
```

Figure 6.10 illustrates the effect that can be achieved by combining overlapping ellipses.

Figure 6.10
Overlapping
Ellipse Elements

```
<ellipse cx="150" cy="150" rx="100" ry="70"
        style="fill:red" />

<ellipse cx="140" cy="100" cx="120" ry="100"
        style="fill:white" />
```

6.2.4 The `line` Element

A line is described by the coordinates of its endpoints (**x1, y2**) and (**x2, y2**). In addition, all of the stroke CSS properties are available to control the physical appearance of the line. Hence, a red line segment from the point (10, 20) to the point (350, 295) could be described by the example in Figure 6.11.

Figure 6.11
The line *Element*

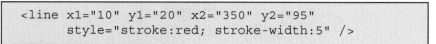

```
<line x1="10" y1="20" x2="350" y2="95"
      style="stroke:red; stroke-width:5" />
```

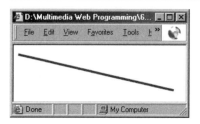

6.2.5 The `polyline` Element

A **polyline** is an open shape created by a series of connected line segments. SVG describes the path of the **polyline** by quoting the coordinates within the **points** attribute. For example, the specification

```
<polyline
  style="stroke:blue; stroke-width: 10; fill:none"
  points="50 150 50 50 350 50 350 150" />
```

describes the series of line segments (50, 150) to (50, 50); followed by (50, 50) to (350, 50); and then finally (350, 50) to (350, 150).

   Note that we have to specify that the CSS **fill** property is set to "**none**". By default, if no fill style is specified, SVG attempts to use a black opaque fill for the interior of the area described by the line segments.

Figure 6.12
The `polyline`
Element

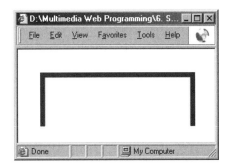

6.2.6 The `polygon` Element

The `polygon` element is specified in exactly the same manner as the `polyline`, except that a line segment is drawn connecting the last point to the first, so creating a closed shape. Figure 6.13 demonstrates the use of the `polygon` element to create a triangle shape.

Figure 6.13
The `polygon`
Element

```
<polygon points="150 20 50 150 250 150"
         style="stroke: red; stroke-width: 5;
                 fill: orange" />
```

6.2.7 The `path` Element

The `path` element is the most powerful of the basic shapes, and can be used to represent any two-dimensional structure as a collection of lines, arcs and curves. The desired shape is specified using a notation that describes the actions of a virtual brush. For example, the series of commands

```
M 100 50 L 200 400
```

would be interpreted by the path element as a *move* (M) to the coordinate position (100, 50) followed by a *line* (L) from that point to the coordinate position (200, 400). The endpoint of the line now becomes the new "current position" from where the next drawing instruction will begin.

If successive commands are the same - for example if we wished to add a second line from (200, 400) to the position (150, 250) - then the command can be omitted. Hence the command sequence

```
M 100 50 L 200 400 150 250
```

would have exactly the same effect as the sequence

```
M 100 50 L 200 400 L 150 250
```

Figure 6.14 illustrates a combination of move and line commands to produce an arrow symbol. As with the **polyline** element, we have to explicitly declare that no **fill** is required.

Figure 6.14
The **path** *Element*

```
<path d="M 80 50 L 140 10 200 50 M 140 180 L 140 10"
      style="stroke:green; stroke-width:6; fill:none" />
```

The **M** and **L** commands in the example above use absolute coordinates to express the destination of moves and the endpoints of lines. We can also express the geometry in relative coordinates by using the lowercase **m** and **l** versions of the commands. In this case, each coordinate position is expressed as the coordinate displacement from the current position. Hence, the arrowhead path of Figure 6.16 could equally be expressed as

```
M 80 50 l 60 -40 60 40 m -60 130 l 0 -170
```

SVG paths also support two kinds of curves —quadratic and cubic Bezier curves.

Quadratic Bezier curves are specified by two endpoints and a single control point that influences the shape of the curve. Figure 6.15 illustrates a quadratic Bezier curve, with circles used to identify the location of the endpoints and control point.

Figure 6.15
Quadratic Bezier Curve

```
<<path d="M 20 150 Q 100 20 180 150"
      style="stroke:red; stroke-width:6; fill:none" />

  <circle cx="20" cy="150" r="10" style="fill:black" />
  <circle cx="100" cy="20" r="10" style="fill:black" />
  <circle cx="180" cy="150" r="10" style="fill:black" />
```

Cubic Bezier curves are specified in a similar way, except that two control points are employed, as illustrated in Figure 6.16.

Figure 6.16
Cubic Bezier Curve

```
<<path d="M 20 150 C 110 20 190 200 180 150"
      style="stroke:red; stroke-width:6; fill:none" />

  <circle cx="20" cy="150" r="10" style="fill:black" />
  <circle cx="110" cy="20" r="10" style="fill:black" />
  <circle cx="190" cy="200" r="10" style="fill:black" />
  <circle cx="280" cy="150" r="10" style="fill:black" />
```

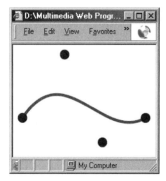

One additional useful path option is the *closepath* command (**z**) that causes a straight line to be drawn from the last coordinate point in the path back to the first point —thus creating an enclosed shape.

Figure 6.17 revisits the quadratic Bezier curve example and adds a *closepath* command to the **path** data.

Figure 6.17
*The **closepath***
Command

```
<<path d="M 20 150 C 110 20 190 200 180 150 Z"
      style="stroke:red; stroke-width:6; fill:none" />

<circle cx="20" cy="150" r="10" style="fill:black" />
<circle cx="110" cy="20" r="10" style="fill:black" />
<circle cx="190" cy="200" r="10" style="fill:black" />
<circle cx="280" cy="150" r="10" style="fill:black" />
```

6.3 Text

6.3.1 Displaying Text

SVG represents text as a sequence of characters, positioned in accordance with **x** and **y** properties, and with the appearance of the text determined by CSS attributes. Figure 6.18 demonstrates the structure of the `<text>` element. Note that, unlike other SVG objects we have met so far, `<text>` is a container element, with the string to be rendered quoted between opening and closing tags.

Figure 6.18
The **text** *Element*

```
<text x="20" y="60"
      style="font-family:Arial font-size:36; stroke:black;
             stroke-width:2; fill:red">
      Using stroke and fill
</text>
<text x="40" y="120"
      style="font-family:Times New Roman; font-size:36;
             stroke:none; fill:red">
      Text with no stroke
</text>
<text x="60" y="180"
      style="font-family:Comic Sans MS; font-size:36;
             stroke:black; stroke-width:2; fill:none">
      Text with no fill
</text>
```

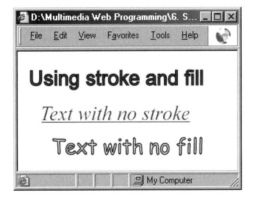

SVG treats text as any other graphic object to be displayed. Hence, the thickness and colour of the text is determined by the `stroke` properties, while the `fill` properties determine the colour and style of the interior of each character. SVG also makes available the full range of CSS text and font properties, so underline (`text-decoration`) and italics (`font-style`) are achievable in the normal way.

179

6.3.2   Text Layout

Text elements are positioned according to the **x** and **y** attributes of the `<text>` element. However, when using text to illustrate other positioned SVG elements, it is important to recognise that the **x** and **y** attributes refer to the bottom left corner of the bounding box of the text object. We should therefore adjust the text coordinates appropriately in accordance with the shape and location of the element to be described.

For example, Figure 6.19 adds text labels to the Quadratic Bezier Curve example of Figure 6.15 so that the coordinate positions of the endpoints and the control point are displayed as text objects.

It is important to recognise the limitations of SVG text when compared to a standard HTML/CSS organisation. In HTML we can define a paragraph element containing an arbitrary piece of text. The text will automatically word-wrap when a line runs out of space in accordance with the available browser space or predefined CSS properties. SVG does not provide such a facility, requiring us to set the line size and to explicitly position each line of text to be displayed.

Figure 6.19
Using Text

```
<path d="M 20 150 Q 150 20 280 150"
      style="stroke:red; stroke-width:6; fill:none" />

<circle cx="20" cy="150" r="10" style="fill:black" />
<circle cx="150" cy="20" r="10" style="fill:black" />
<circle cx="280" cy="150" r="10" style="fill:black" />

<text x="30" y="170"
      style="fill:rgb(0,0,128); font-family:arial;
            font-size:18">
      (20, 150)
</text>

 <text x="165" y="25"
      style="fill:rgb(0,0,128); font-family:arial;
            font-size: 18">
      (150, 20)
 </text>

<text x="200" y="180"
      style="fill:rgb(0,0,128); font-family:arial;
            font-size:18">
      (280, 150)
</text>
```

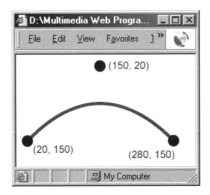

On the other hand, when compared to text within a bitmap image, SVG exhibits significant advantages. SVG text remains in ASCII format even after it is incorporated into a SVG image. This makes it available for indexing by search engines, and also enables us to highlight text within a SVG image, so that we can copy and paste it into some other application.

When laying out text in SVG, we frequently wish to make a local modification to the appearance of a section of the text, while remaining within the current text element. The **<tspan>** element enables us to perform such adjustments. For example, consider Figure 6.20 where a **<tspan>** element is used to modify the style of a single word with a **<text>** element.

Figure 6.20
The **tspan** *Element*

```
<text x="20" y="50"
    style="fill:blue; font-family:arial; font-size:24">
  Using the
    <tspan style="font-weight:bold; fill:red">
            tspan
    </tspan>
  element.
</text>
```

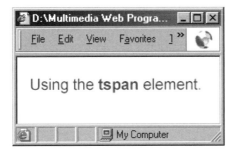

Note how the **<tspan>** element provides local style information to be applied to the text contained within the span. All other styles are inherited from the **<text>** element. Where the **<tspan>** style definition conflicts with that of the **<text>** element (for example, the **fill** colour), then the **<tspan>** definition takes precedence.

The **<tspan>** element also allows us to use relative positioning to adjust the current text position horizontally and vertically within a text element. This can be particularly useful when positioning a passage of text which spans multiple lines. Consider the example below, where a single **<text>** element is presented as a collection of **<tspan>** elements.

Figure 6.21
Multiple **tspan**
Elements

```
<text style="fill:blue; font-family:arial; font-size:24">
   <tspan x="10" y="30">
      The &lt;tspan&gt; element allows us to </tspan>
   <tspan x="10" dy="1.5em">
      use relative positioning to adjust </tspan>
   <tspan x="10" dy="1.5em">
      the current text position horizontally </tspan>
   <tspan x="10" dy="1.5em">
      and vertically within an element. </tspan>
</text>
```

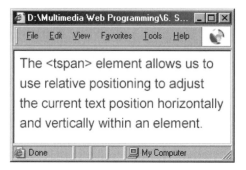

Here, the paragraph (**<text>** element) is organised as a series of lines (**<tspan>** elements), where each **<tspan>** has its position explicitly set, and each inherits its presentation style from the surrounding **<text>** element. Note that only the first **<tspan>** has an absolute (**x**, **y**) coordinate position set —the others have an absolute x-coordinate set, but the y-coordinate is expressed relative to the y-coordinate of the previous **<tspan>** using the **dy** attribute.

Since the paragraph is contained within a single `<text>` element, it can be highlighted (and subsequently copied) as a single entity.

Using relative positioning also makes it easier to reposition a block of text on the canvas. If, for example, we wanted to move the paragraph in Figure 6.21 down the canvas by 100 pixels, we could simply change the `y` attribute of the first `<tspan>` element. All other `<tspan>` elements would maintain their position relative to the first one.

6.4 More Complex SVG Structures

6.4.1 Groups

The group (`<g>`) element allows us to collect together a number of SVG primitives and treat them as a single component. This is particularly useful when we want to construct a logo or menu, where we require a certain style to be applied (or modified) globally to a collection of primitives.

Figure 6.22 illustrates a simple group comprising a `<rect>`, `<ellipse>` and `<text>` element, where style information applied to the group is inherited by each of the group members.

Figure 6.22
Grouping Elements

```
<g style="fill:blue; stroke:black; stroke-width:2">

    <rect x="50" y="50" width="300" height="50" />

    <text style="font-size:48; font-family:arial">
        <tspan x="120" y="150">Defining</tspan>
        <tspan x="190" dy="1em">a</tspan>
        <tspan x="145" dy="1em">group</tspan>
        <tspan x="155" dy="1em">style</tspan>
    </text>

  <ellipse cx="200" cy="200" rx="180" ry="130"
          style="fill-opacity:0.3" />

</g>
```

6.4.2 Applying Transformations

One of the main advantages of grouping elements is that we can then apply transformations to the group as a single element. SVG supplies four specific transformations —*translation*, *scaling*, *rotation* and *skew*, plus a general-purpose *matrix* transformation, as described below.

`translate (tx, ty)`	Create a new coordinate system for the group with its origin at the coordinate point (`tx`, `ty`) in the original system. This transformation has the effect of shifting the group by `tx` units in the horizontal direction and by `ty` units in the vertical direction.
`scale (s)`	Create a new coordinate system for the group, which is scaled by a factor of `s` from the original.
`rotate (r, rx, ry)`	Create a new coordinate system for the group, which is rotated by `r` degrees about the coordinate point (`rx`, `ry`) in the current system. If no values for `rx` and `ry` are specified, then the rotation is about the origin of the original coordinate system.
`skewX (s)`	Create a new coordinate system for the group, which is skewed by `s` degrees in the x direction from the original.

`skewY (s)`	Create a new coordinate system for the group, which is skewed by **s** degrees in the y direction from the original.
`matrix (a,b,c,d,e,f)`	Create a new coordinate system for the group, which is defined by applying the transformation matrix (**a,b,c,d,e,f**) to the original system.

Transformations are applied to groups (or to individual objects) by the **transform** attribute as illustrated by Figure 6.23, which demonstrates translation, rotation and scaling.

Figure 6.23
Using
Transformations

```
<g>
    <path d="M 20 30 L 180 30 M 160 10 L 180 30 L 160 50"
        style="stroke:blue; stroke-width:2;
                fill:none" />

    <text x="25" y="50"
        style="font-size:16; font-family:verdana;
                stroke:none; fill:black">
        Transformations
    </text>
</g>


<g transform="translate(100, 100) rotate(45) scale(1.5)">
    <path d="M 20 30 L 180 30 M 160 10 L 180 30 L 160 50"
        style="stroke:blue; stroke-width:2;
                fill:none" />

    <text x="25" y="50"
        style="font-size:16; font-family:verdana;
                stroke:none; fill:black">
        Transformations
    </text>
</g>
```

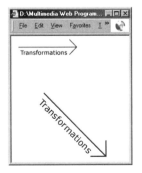

185

This example defines two identical symbols as groups, each created from a `<path>` element and a `<text>` element. Note that the coordinate data are identical in each case.

The second group, however, also specifies a series of transformations that define, for that group, a new coordinate system which is translated by 100 pixels in each direction, rotated around its origin, and then scaled by a factor of 150% with respect to the original. The graphic elements in this group are then rendered according to the new coordinate system, resulting in the larger of the graphic symbols shown.

6.4.3   Reusing Code

The previous example illustrated a pair of identical objects, presented in different ways by using transformations. The SVG `<symbol>` element enables us to provide a single definition for such objects so that they can be easily reused by referring to the original definition.

Figure 6.24 illustrates how the previous example could be more economically defined by using the `<symbol>` element.

Figure 6.24
Using the `symbol`
Element

```
<symbol id="myArrow">
   <path d="M 20 30 L 180 30 M 160 10 L 180 30 L 160 50"
         style="stroke:blue; stroke-width:2; fill:none" />
   <text x="25" y="50"
         style="font-size:16; font-family:verdana;
                stroke:none; fill:black">
      Transformations
   </text>
</symbol>

<use xlink:href="#myArrow" />

<g transform="translate(100, 100) rotate(45) scale(1.5)">
   <use xlink:href="#myArrow" />
</g>
```

In order to use the symbol, we simply refer to it by name (the `id` property assigned when the symbol was created) within the `xlink:href` property of the `<use>` element. In this example, we use the symbol twice —once in its default coordinate system, and again after a series of transformations. In order to apply the transformations, we enclose the second **<use>** element within a group.

Note that the **<symbol>** element does not cause anything to be drawn to the canvas —it merely creates the definition for later reference from a **<use>** element.

SVG also provides a **<defs>** element for creating general definitions for later reuse. This has more general applications than **<symbol>**, and can be used to specify fills and patterns that can then be applied to later elements; but it can also be used to create symbols if desired.

Figure 6.25 recreates the example of 6.23 using the **<defs>** element.

Figure 6.25

Using the <defs> Element

```
<defs>
   <g id="myArrow">
      <path d="M 20 30 L 180 30 M 160 10 L 180 30 L 160 50"
         style="stroke:blue; stroke-width:2; fill:none" />

      <text x="25" y="50"
            style="font-size:16; font-family:verdana;
                   stroke:none; fill:black">
            Transformations
      </text>
   </g>
</defs>

<use xlink:href="#myArrow" />

<g transform="translate(100, 100) rotate(45) scale(1.5)">
   <use xlink:href="#myArrow" />
</g>
```

The **<defs>** tag provides a container where elements can be defined for future reference. Unlike **<symbol>**, which can only be used to create graphical objects, **<defs>** allows us to also define various effects and styles. In this case, we enclose the components of the object being defined within a **<g>** element, so that it can be used as a single entity.

6.4.4   Reusing Text

The previous two examples have demonstrated how the `<use>` element can be employed to reference a graphical object defined by the `<defs>` and `<symbol>` tags. SVG also supports reuse of text through the `<tref>` tag, which is used in a similar manner to `<use>`.

The text to be displayed is specified in a `<text>` element located within a `<def>` element. The `<text>` element includes an `id` attribute that is used by the `<tref>` element to link to the text to be displayed.

Figure 6.26 presents a simple example, in which a message created in a `<defs>` element is referenced by a pair of `<tref>` elements that apply two different presentation styles to the message. Note how the `<tref>` element is contained within a `<text>` container, which can apply all the usual style and position information.

Figure 6.26
Using the `<tref>`
Element

```
<defs>
   <text id="myMessage">
      One message, but two different styles
   </text>
</defs>

<text x="80" y="40"
      style="font-family:verdana; font-size:16;
             fill:navy; stroke:none">
      <tref xlink:href="#myMessage" />
</text>

<text x="15" y="100"
      style="font-family:'comic sans ms'; font-size:28;
             font-style:italics; fill:lime; stroke:black;
             stroke-width:1">
      <tref xlink:href="#myMessage" />
</text>
```

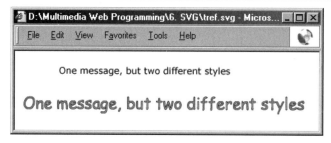

188

We can combine the various methods of code and text reuse to implement text positioned along a path, as illustrated by Figure 6.27 below.

We first define a `<path>` element along which the text will flow by enclosing it within in a `<defs>` section. This path will be referenced to draw the path and also to fit the text along it. Later in the page, the `<text>` element sets the style in which the text is to be displayed, while a nested `<textpath>` element references the path along which the text is placed.

Figure 6.27
Fitting Text Along a Path

```
<defs> <path id="myPath"
            d="M 20 200 C 50 0 300 400 380 150" />
</defs>

<use xlink:href="#myPath"
    style="fill:none; stroke:pink; stroke-width:2" />

<text style="font-family:verdana; fill:black; stroke:none;
            font-size: 24">
   <textPath xlink:href="#myPath">
       Fitting text along a predefined path
   </textPath>
</text>
```

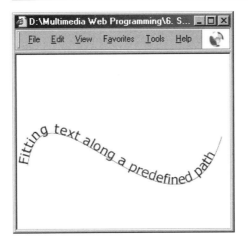

6.5 Advanced Fills – Using Gradients and Patterns

We have seen how we use the `fill` and `opacity` properties to specify the interior colour of any SVG element that bounds a finite space. This section introduces gradients and patterns, which enable us to apply a more sophisticated appearance to these elements.

6.5.1 Using Gradients

A gradient is a smooth transition from one colour to another. In SVG, we create named gradient elements in the **<defs>** section of the document. We can then apply the gradient to elements by referring to the gradient by name in the elements **fill** style property.

SVG supports two types of gradient element. Linear gradients are transitions that are applied horizontally (left to right), vertically (top-to-bottom) or diagonally (at an angle between the horizontal and vertical). Radial gradients are applied from a point in the interior of the element towards the perimeter.

Figure 6.28 illustrates the definition of a simple transition from red to blue as a horizontal linear gradient, and its application to a text element. Note that linear gradients are horizontal by default. We will later see how to create vertical and diagonal gradients.

Figure 6.28
Using the
linearGradient
Element

```
<defs>
    <linearGradient id="myGradient">
        <stop offset="0%" style="stop-color: yellow" />
        <stop offset="100%" style="stop-color: navy" />
    </linearGradient>
</defs>

<text x="10" y="80"
    style="font-family:'comic sans ms'; font-size:36;
        stroke:none; fill:url(#myGradient)">
    My first gradient fill
</text>
```

190

The colours to be used in the gradient are defined within the `<linearGradient>` tag as `<stop>` elements. The `offset` property determines the point within the gradient at which the named `stop-color` is reached. For example, in Figure 6.29, we have defined a red `<stop>` element at a gradient `offset` of 0% (the left hand edge of the gradient), and a blue `<stop>` element at a gradient `offset` of 100% (the right hand edge of the gradient).

We apply the gradient to an object by referring to it by name (the gradient's **id** property) with the syntax

```
url(#myGradient)
```

where `url` (...) indicates a pointer reference to an XML element and `#myGradient` refers to the element in the current document with an **id** attribute of "*myGradient*".

The colour of each point in the object is then generated by a weighted mix of the *stop colours* (red and blue), with the quantity of each colour controlled by the location with respect to the offset of each stop colour.

6.5.2 More Linear Gradients

It is possible to specify a gradient of more than two colours by specifying a `<stop>` element for each colour required. The `offset` property of each `<stop>` element controls which pair of colours are combined at any point within the gradient. For example, Figure 6.29 illustrates a gradient from yellow to red and then to cyan, applied to a `<rect>` element. Here, the left half of the `<rect>` is a gradient from yellow to red (where the `offset` is in the range 0% to 50%), and the right half of the `<rect>` is a gradient from red to cyan (where the `offset` is in the range 50% to 100%).

Figure 6.29
Multi-coloured
Gradients

```
<defs>
    <linearGradient id="myGradient">
        <stop offset="0%" style="stop-color:yellow" />
        <stop offset="50%" style="stop-color:red" />
        <stop offset="100%" style="stop-color:cyan" />
    </linearGradient>
</defs>

<rect x="10" y="10" width="380" height="380"
      style="fill:url(#myGradient)" />
```

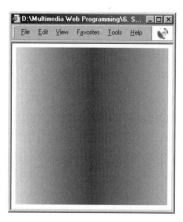

All of our examples so far have been horizontal gradients, running from left to right along the interior of an element. In order to specify gradients in other directions, we need to specify a gradient vector by setting **x1, y1** and **x2, y2** attributes for the `<linearGradient>` element.

The values **x1, y1, x2** and **y2** can be thought of as the corners of a unit box, where (0, 0) specifies the top-left corner; (0, 1) is the bottom-left corner; (1,0) is the top-right corner and (1,1) is the bottom-right corner. By assigning (**x1, y1**) and (**x2, y2**) to a pair of corner positions, we create a vector (**x1, y1**) → (**x2, y2**) which describes the direction of the gradient. For example, the assignment **x1**=0, **y1**=0, **x2**=0, **y1**=1 describes the vector from top-left (0,0) to bottom-left (0,1), hence the gradient will run vertically from top to bottom (vector *a*, below). Alternatively, the assignment **x1**=0, **y1**=0, **x2**=1, **y2**=1 describes the vector from top-left to bottom-right, hence the gradient will run diagonally from top to bottom and left to right (vector *b*, below).

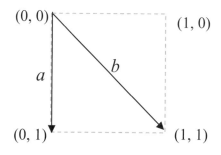

Figure 6.30 illustrates the specification and application of the gradient described by vector *a*, above. Note that an identical gradient could also be specified by the assignment `x1`=1, `y1`=0, `x2`=1, `y2`=1 —hence the vector from top-right to bottom-right.

Figure 6.30
Vertical Gradient

```
<defs>
   <linearGradient id="myGradient"
         x1="0" y1="0" x2="0" y2="1">
      <stop offset="0%" style="stop-color:red" />
      <stop offset="100%" style="stop-color:yellow" />
   </linearGradient>
</defs>

<rect x="10" y="10" width="380" height="380"
      style="fill: url(#myGradient)" />
```

The gradient described by vector *b* is presented in Figure 6.31.

Figure 6.31
Diagonal Gradient

```
<defs>
   <linearGradient id="myGradient"
         x1="0" y1="0" x2="1" y2="1">
      <stop offset="0%" style="stop-color:red" />
      <stop offset="100%" style="stop-color:yellow" />
   </linearGradient>
</defs>

<rect x="10" y="10" width="380" height="380"
      style="fill: url(#myGradient)" />
```

6.5.3 Radial Gradients

A radial gradient is one where the centre of the gradient (where the offset is deemed to be 0%) is determined by the coordinate point described by attributes **cx** and **cy**. The gradient moves out in all directions for a distance defined by the attribute **r** (the radius of the circle describing the extent of the gradient).

Figure 6.32 illustrates a radial gradient from red to blue applied to a **<rect>** element, with the centre of the gradient at the coordinate point (200, 200). The radius of the gradient is defined to be 200 pixels, so that the area covered by the gradient fits neatly inside the **<rect>**. Note that the inclusion of the attribute assignment

```
gradientUnits=userSpaceOnUse
```

enables us to specify gradient attributes using the same coordinate system as that used to specify the box. We could alternatively have used

```
gradientUnits=objectBoundingBox
```

which enables us to express gradient coordinates relative to the origin of the bounding box of the object to which the gradient is to be applied.

Figure 6.32
Radial Gradient

```
<defs>
    <radialGradient id="myGradient"
            gradientUnits=userSpaceOnUse
            cx="200" cy="200" r="200">
        <stop offset="0%"
              style="stop-color:red; stop-opacity:1" />
        <stop offset="100%"
              style="stop-color:blue; stop-opacity:0" />
    </radialGradient>
</defs>

<rect x="10" y="10" width="380" height="380"
    style="fill:url(#myGradient);
            stroke:black; stroke-width:2" />
```

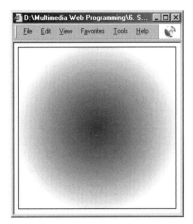

Note also that we have assigned a **stop-opacity** attribute as well as a **stop-color** attribute for each **<stop>** element. In this case we specify that the fill is completely opaque (**opacity**=1) at the centre of the gradient (**offset**=0%), with its opacity diminishing along the extent of the gradient until it is completely transparent (**opacity**=0) at the extreme (**offset**=100%). The **stop-opacity** attribute can also be specified for linear gradients, and enables us to achieve a wide range of subtle effects.

6.5.4   Using Patterns

A pattern is an image that is tiled across the interior of an SVG element when used as the object of a **fill** attribute, or used to trace the outline of an SVG element when used as the object of a **stroke**

195

element. Patterns are specified in the **\<defs\>** section of the document and are referenced by their id attribute in the same way as for gradients. Figure 6.33 illustrates the definition of a simple triangle pattern and its application across a **\<rect\>** element.

As for gradients, the attribute **patternUnits** defines the coordinate system for attributes **x**, **y**, **width** and **height**. Attribute values **userSpaceOnUse** and **objectBoundingBox** are both available, and have the same effect as described earlier.

In this example, we define the pattern canvas as an area of 100 x 100 pixels on the browser, with an upper left coordinate of (0, 0). In addition, the **viewBox** attribute defines that this pattern canvas is to be represented by a coordinate system with values from (0, 0) to (100, 100). We then use a **\<path\>** element to define the outline of a triangle to be rendered using a green **stroke** and yellow **fill**.

The defined pattern is then applied to the **fill** style property of a **\<rect\>** element by tiling the triangle pattern across the element's interior.

Figure 6.33
Using Patterns

```
<defs>
    <pattern id="myPattern" patternUnits="userSpaceOnUse"
          x="0" y="0" width="100" height="100"
          viewBox="0 0 100 100">
        <path d="M 50 30 L 30 80 70 80 Z"
            style="stroke:green; stroke-width:2;
                   fill: yellow" />
    </pattern>
</defs>

<rect x="10" y="10" width="380" height="380"
      style="stroke:black; fill:url(#myPattern)" />
```

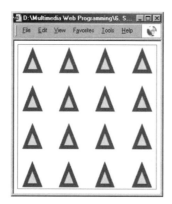

196

6.6 Filter Effects

6.6.1 SVG Filters

SVG filters comprise a set of graphics operations that are applied to a source graphic to provide a modified graphic result. A range of filters is available, and these can be connected in series to create a wide range of different effects.

In SVG, filters are defined within the **<defs>** section of the document, by enclosing the filter definition within a **<filter>** tag. Each **<filter>** element contains a set of *filter primitives*, each of which performs a single graphical operation, controlled by a set of attributes. Figure 6.34 illustrates the *Gaussian Blur* filter applied to a text element.

Figure 6.34
A First Filter

```
<defs>
  <filter id="myBlur">
    <feGaussianBlur in="SourceGraphic" stdDeviation="3" />
  </filter>
</defs>

<text x="10" y="50"
    style="filter:url(#myBlur); font-family:verdana;
           font-size:48; stroke:none; fill:red">
    Using a filter
</text>
```

The Gaussian Blur filter is specified by the **<feGaussianBlur>** element, which applies a blurring effect to the source graphic. The extent of the blur is determined by the **stdDeviation** (standard deviation) property. The **in** attribute specifies that the subject of the blur effect is the element to which the effect is to be applied. Other options for **in** will be introduced later.

The filter is applied by setting the **filter** style property of the target element (in this case the **<text>** element). This is done by referring to the **url** of the filter's **id** property as we have already done for gradients and patterns.

6.6.2   Using Filters: Creating a Drop Shadow

The Gaussian Blur filter is commonly used to apply a drop shadow effect to text elements by creating a blurred shadow and rendering it below the plain text element, offset by a small amount. This is illustrated by Figure 6.35.

Figure 6.35
Text with a Drop
Shadow

```
<defs>
   <filter id="dropShadow">
     <feGaussianBlur in="SourceAlpha"
          stdDeviation="2" result="blurredText" />
     <feOffset in="blurredText" dx="4" dy="4"
               result="offsetBlur" />
     <feMerge> <feMergeNode in="offsetBlur" />
               <feMergeNode in="SourceGraphic" />
     </feMerge>
   </filter>
</defs>

<text x="10" y="100"
      style="filter:url(#dropShadow); font-family:verdana;
            font-size: 48; stroke:none; fill:red">
     Using a filter
</text>
```

This example presents the generation of drop shadow text as a 3-stage process.

First, we specify the Gaussian Blur filter. This time, note that the `in` attribute is `sourceAlpha` rather than `sourceGraphic`. This has the effect of generating a blurred monochrome representation of the original graphic element, rather than the coloured version from the original example. The `<feGaussianBlur>` element also has a `result` attribute set, providing a name by which the result of the blur can be passed forward to the next stage of the process.

Next, we use the `<feOffset>` element to displace the shadow from the position of the original text. The exact `dx` and `dy` values used will depend on the direction in which the shadow is cast, and the depth of shadow required. Note that the `in` attribute of the `<feOffset>` element corresponds to the result generated by the `<feGaussianBlur>`.

Finally, we use the `<feMerge>` element to generate a single graphical image consisting of the text to be presented (`sourceGraphic`) and the offset, blurred shadow (the `result` of the `<feMerge>`). The order of the components within the `<feMerge>` is important, since SVG will render elements in the order in which they appear in the code. As we want the shadow to appear *underneath* the text, we must make sure that it is drawn *first*.

6.6.3 Lighting Models

One of the most powerful uses of SVG filters is to apply complex lighting models to scenes. We can specify single or multiple light sources, model specular and diffuse illumination, and merge or blend the effects of multiple effects.

Figure 6.36 implements a more complex example that applies specular illumination and drop shadow filters to a `<rect>` element to create a metallic three-dimensional button object.

Figure 6.36
Illumination Filter
Effects

```
<defs>
   <filter id="shiny3d">
      <feGaussianBlur in="SourceAlpha"
                  stdDeviation="2" result="blurred" />
      <feOffset in="blurred" dx="5" dy="5"
               result="offsetBlurred" />
      <feSpecularLighting in="blurred" surfaceScale="6"
                           specularConstant="0.8"
                           specularExponent="15"
                           lighting-color="white"
                           result="specularOut">
          <feDistantLight azimuth="225" elevation="30" />
      </feSpecularLighting>
      <feComposite in="specularOut" in2="SourceAlpha"
            operator="in" result="specularOutShadow" />
      <feComposite in="SourceGraphic"
                  in2="specularOutShadow"
                  operator="arithmetic"
                  k1="0" k2="1" k3="1" k4="0"
                  result="shinyButton" />
      <feMerge>
          <feMergeNode in="offsetBlurred" />
          <feMergeNode in="shinyButton" />
      </feMerge>
   </filter>
</defs>

<g style="filter:url(#shiny3d)">
<rect x="20" y="20" rx="10" ry="10"
      width="180" height="50"
      style="fill: blue; stroke:none" />
<text x="110" y="55"
      style="font-family:verdana; font-size:24;
            stroke:none; fill:white; text-anchor:middle">
      Click here
</text>
</g>
```

Figure 6.36 defines a `<filter>` that combines a drop shadow
with specular illumination to create the illusion of a three-

dimensional object with a shiny metallic finish. The filter is constructed according to the following steps.

1. A drop shadow is created using the `<feGaussianBlur>` and `<feOffset>` elements.

2. The `<feSpecularLighting>` primitive defines a light source to be applied to the height map represented by the result of the Gaussian Blur. The primitive is controlled by a number of attributes: `surfaceScale` determines the height of the interior of the object; `specularConstant` is a value in the range 0...1 and defines the brightness of the reflection; `specularExponent` is a value in the range 1...128 and is used to determine how "shiny" the resultant object is; and `lighting-color` determines the colour of the light source.

3. The `<feDistantLight>` primitive applies a light source to the scene. The `azimuth` attribute expresses the direction in degrees of the light source. A value of 225 in this example positions the light source to the top-left of the element — corresponding with the direction of the drop shadow. The `elevation` attribute defines the height of the light source.

4. We now wish to combine the various primitives specified so far. The `<feComposite>` primitive combines a pair of input images according to some combination rule. In this instance, we combine the result of the `<feSpecularReflection>` primitive with the *alpha plane* of the source image (an intensity map of the image) using the `in` rule; and then combine this result with the original image using the `arithmetic` rule.

The filter is applied to a "flat" button object created from a blue `<rect>` and some white `<text>`. The original image is shown on the left in Figure 6.36. As we want to apply the filter to the combined graphic, we create a group by enclosing the `<rect>` and `<text>` within a `<g>` element. We then apply the filter to the `<g>`, obtaining the result shown on the right in Figure 6.36.

6.7 Interactive SVG

6.7.1 Scripting in SVG

SVG includes the `<script>` element, which provides a similar functionality to HTML scripting. In addition, each SVG element responds to the usual events `onclick`, `onmouseover`, `onmouseout`, and `onload` (among other events). Figure 6.37 illustrates an event handler for the `onclick` event, which triggers the modification of a pair of SVG element attributes.

Figure 6.37
Event-Driven SVG

```
<script type="text/javascript">
  function moveBox(evt) {
    var theBox = evt.target;
    var currentX = parseInt(theBox.getAttribute("x"));
    var currentY = parseInt(theBox.getAttribute("y"));
    theBox.setAttribute("x", currentX+150);
    theBox.setAttribute("y", currentY+100);
  }
</script>

<rect onclick="moveBox(evt)"
      x="50" y="50" width="100" height="100"
      style="fill: yellow; fill-opacity: 1" />

<text x="200" y="350"
      style="font-family: Arial; font-size: 24;
             text-anchor: middle">
  Click on the box to make it jump
</text>
```

Figure 6.37 presents a `<rect>` element for which an **onclick** event handler is specified. The parameter passed to the handler is a handle to the event that has been triggered. The SVG DOM provides **getAttribute** and **setAttribute** methods that allow us to gain access to individual attributes of SVG elements; we use these in this example to modify the **x** and **y** properties of the `<rect>` element in response to a mouse click.

6.7.2   Event Handling

Although the scripting approach illustrated in Figure 6.37 is attractive to developers with experience of DHTML and JavaScript, SVG also provides a much more flexible approach to specifying event-driven interactive applications.

Figure 6.38 presents a dynamic menu, where option buttons change appearance when the mouse cursor passes over them. Each option is enclosed in a named `<a>` element, which has a similar structure and effect as the corresponding element in HTML.

Each menu button consists of a rounded `<rect>` element and some `<text>`. Within each of these, a `<set>` element is used to animate the **fill** attribute in response to specified events. Note that the `<rect>` element must be expressed as a container element (i.e. `<rect>` ... `</rect>`) to enable this.

In the case of the `<rect>`, the **fill** attribute is set to *white* when the mouse moves over the hyperlink (the area covered by the `<a>`). When the mouse moves off the hyperlink, then the **fill** attribute is returned to its original state. The `<set>` within the `<text>` element operates in the same way, except that the colour changes from *white* to *navy*.

The leftmost image in Figure 6.38 represents the initial state of the menu, where all buttons are rendered with white text on a navy background. When the cursor is moved over the top button (*Option 1*), then the event handlers for the `<rect>` and `<text>` elements modify the respective **fill** attributes, resulting in the image on the right. When the cursor moves away from the button again, then **fill** attributes are restored to their initial state.

Figure 6.38
Animated Menu with
Mouseover Effects

```
<a id="myLink1" xlink:href="option1.svg">
<rect x="50" y="50" height="40" width="200"
      rx="20" ry="20"
      style="fill:navy; stroke:navy; stroke-width:3">
      <set attributeName="fill" to="white"
           begin="myLink1.mouseover"
           end="myLink1.mouseout" />
</rect>
<text x="150" y="78"
      style="font-size:24; fill:white; stroke:none;
             text-anchor:middle">
      <set attributeName="fill" to="navy"
           begin="myLink1.mouseover"
           end="myLink1.mouseout" />
   Option 1
</text>
</a>

<!-- similar code for Option 2 and Option 3 goes here -->
```

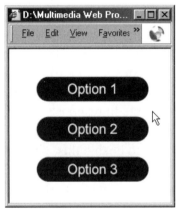
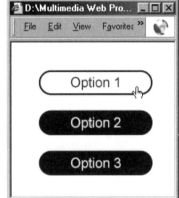

6.8   Animated SVG

6.8.1   Specifying Animation

SVG provides a very powerful `<animate>` element that enables us to define time-based modifications to element attributes. Figure 6.39 illustrates a pair of `<rect>` elements for which the `width` attribute is animated, causing the rectangle to stretch over time. The images presented demonstrate three stages in the progress of the animation.

Figure 6.39
Interpolated
Animation

```
<rect x="10" y="50" height="10" width="0"
      style="fill:red; stroke:none">
   <animate attributeName="width" from="0" to="250"
            dur="5s" repeatCount="indefinite" />
</rect>

<rect x="10" y="100" height="10" width="0"
      style="fill:blue; stroke:none">
   <animate attributeName="width"
            values="0; 20; 50; 100; 250"
            dur="5s" repeatCount="indefinite" />
</rect>
```

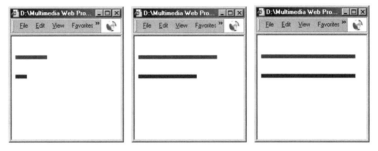

The `<animate>` element is specified within the element to which the animation is applied. The animation for the red rectangle (the first `<rect>` element) is governed by the following parameters.

`attributeName="width"`

Specifies the property of the element to be animated. If more than one attribute of an element is to be animated, then a separate `<animate>` tag is required for each.

`from="0" to="250"`

Specifies the range of values to be applied to the named attribute.

`dur="5s"`

Controls the speed of the animation by specifying the time in seconds that will be taken to move between the values `from` and `to`.

`repeatCount="indefinite"`

Specifies that the animation should repeat continuously. If a numeric value is provided for `repeatCount` (e.g.

`repeatCount="5"`), then the animation would loop for that number of times.

The animation of the `width` for the blue rectangle (the second `<rect>` element) is specified in the same way as the first, except that a `values` attribute is presented instead of `from` and `to`. This enables us to vary the rate at which the animation proceeds, as follows.

When `from` and `to` attributes are provided, the intermediate stages of the animation are calculated by a simple linear interpolation function, controlled by the time spent so far relative to the value of the `dur` attribute. For example, the `width` of the red `<rect>` will animate between 0 and 250, over a period of 5 seconds. Thus, in each second of the animation, the `width` will grow by 50 pixels.

When a `values` attribute is provided, we identify a series of interpolations to be carried out. For example, the `width` of the blue `<rect>` will be animated according to the values 0, 20, 50, 100 and 250. This identifies four *animation intervals* 0-20, 20-50, 50-100 and 100-250, which will be allocated equal portions of the duration of the animation. For a `dur` of 5 seconds, each interval will be allocated 1.25 seconds. Thus, during the first 1.25 seconds, the `width` will be interpolated between 0 and 20. In the next 1.25 seconds, the `width` will vary between 20 and 50. As each interval covers a greater range of values, the animation will appear to begin slowly and gather pace as it proceeds.

The images in Figure 6.39 illustrate the progress of the animation. The leftmost image represents an early stage in the animation, where the `width` of the upper rectangle is growing at a faster rate than that of the lower rectangle. In the middle image, the lower rectangle is beginning to catch up as its rate of animation increases. By the end of the cycle (after 5 seconds) the `width` of both rectangles reaches the final value of 250 at the same time.

6.8.2   Timed Animation

The previous example presented a pair of animations with a timed duration, where the animations begin as soon as the page had loaded.

The SVG `<animate>` element allows us to chain animations by specifying for each a start time relative to the time at which the page is loaded.

Figure 6.40 presents a scene where the locations of a red box and blue circle are controlled by three animations —one each for the `x` and `y` coordinate attributes of the box, and another for the `cx` coordinate attribute of the circle.

The first `<animate>` element to take effect is that which operates on the `y` attribute of the box. This animation has no `start` attribute specified, so it begins as soon as the page loads. Hence, the initial movement of the box is vertical down the page.

After one second, the `<animate>` element on the x-coordinate attribute of the box is activated. At this point, both the `x` and `y` attributes are subject to animations, so the path of movement of the box changes from vertical to diagonal in a top-to-bottom and left-to-right direction. Both box animations are timed to finish 4 seconds after the initial page load event.

Finally, after a further 2 seconds (3 seconds after the page has loaded), the `<animate>` element on the `cx` attribute of the circle is activated. The circle then sets off from left to right across the screen. As this animation has a duration of 3 seconds, it continues for a further 2 seconds after the box has come to rest.

Figure 6.40 presents three snapshots of the animated sequence as follows:

left: the initial vertical movement of the box
middle: the box moves diagonally while the circle moves from left to right
right: the final state of the animation

Note that all three `<animate>` elements have a `fill` attribute specified. The value of this attribute determines how the scene is presented at the end of the animation. The default behaviour is for the display to revert to the initial state of the scene (i.e. to undo the effect of the animation). Setting the `fill` attribute to `"freeze"` preserves the final state of the animated attribute.

Figure 6.40
Timed Animation

```
<rect x="10" y="10" height="100" width="100"
      style="fill:none; stroke:red; stroke-width:3">
    <animate attributeName="x" to="250"
             begin="1s" dur="3s"
             fill="freeze" />
    <animate attributeName="y" to="250" dur="4s"
             fill="freeze" />
</rect>

<circle cx="80" cy="300" r="40"
        style="fill:blue; stroke:none">
    <animate attributeName="cx" to="300"
             begin="3s" dur="3s" fill="freeze" />
</circle>
```

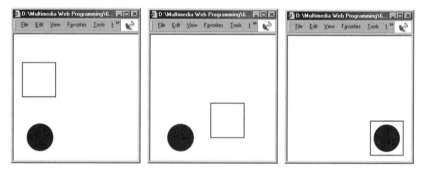

6.8.3   Staged Animation

In addition to specifying the start time of an animation relative to the time at which the page loads, we can specify timed animations relative to the beginning or end of other animations on the page. Figure 6.41 presents a more complex animation, as follows:

1. When the page loads, a text label is presented on the bottom of the canvas. At the same time, a red box begins to stretch across the top of the canvas.
2. When the box has reached its full extent, there is a 2-second gap, after which the text moves up the screen, resting when it is located inside the box.
3. As soon as the text arrives in the box, the interior of the box becomes yellow.
4. After a further 1 second delay, both the text and box begin to move down the canvas.

5. The text and box come to rest, where the final state of the animation is preserved.

The images in Figure 6.41 present four snapshots from the animated sequence.

Figure 6.41
Staged Animation

```
<rect x="10" y="10" height="40" width="0"
      style="fill:none; stroke:red; stroke-width:3">
    <animate id="boxAnim" attributeName="width" to="385"
             dur="3s" fill="freeze" />
    <set attributeName="fill" to="yellow"
             begin="textMove.end" fill="freeze" />
    <animate attributeName="y" to="200"
             begin="textMove.end+1s" dur="1s"
             fill="freeze" />
</rect>

<text x="200" y="350"
      style="font-family:verdana; font-size:24;
             stroke:none; fill:purple; text-
anchor:middle">
    <animate id="textMove" attributeName="y"
             begin="boxAnim.end+2s" to="37"
             dur="2s" fill="freeze" />
    <animate attributeName="y" to="227"
             begin="textMove.end+1s" dur="1s"
             fill="freeze" />
    Animation!!!!!
</text>
```

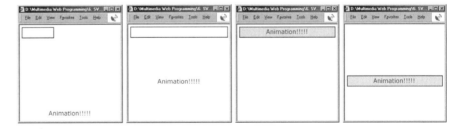

We can specify this sequence by defining the timed relationships between the animations. By assigning an **id** attribute to an **<animate>** element, we can refer to the **begin** or **end** time in subsequent animations.

For example, in Figure 6.41 we require the **<text>** element to start moving up the screen (stage 2, above) 2 seconds after the animation that stretches the **<rect>** element is complete. We

209

achieve this by assigning an `id` of `"boxAnim"` to the *box stretch* animation, and then assigning a value of `"boxAnim.end+2s"` to the `begin` attribute of the *text move* animation. Examining the code in Figure 6.41 reveals similar relationships.

6.8.4 Using `animateMotion`

The `<animate>` element can be regarded as a general-purpose tool that enables us to control the animation of any attribute of an element —whether related to position, colour, opacity, or any other physical characteristic. However, SVG also provides a collection of animation elements that provide greater flexibility for specific types of animation.

We have already seen how we can control the position of an element by combining separate animations for the values of the x and y coordinate attributes. The `<animateMotion>` element provides us with a more powerful option whereby we can specify a path for the animation.

Figure 6.42 presents an application of the `<animateMotion>` element, which describes the animation of a `<rect>` element along the path of a Cubic Bezier curve. The route of the animation can be any path that can be expressed in SVG. Here we specify that the `<rect>` will repeatedly follow the same `<path>`, with a period of 5 seconds.

When animating the position of SVG elements, it is important to remember that it is the reference point of the object that will follow the specified route. This reference point varies with different classes of element. For example, with `<text>` elements, the reference point is the bottom-left corner of the bounding box of the text; with `<circle>` elements, the reference point is the centre of the circle; while for `<rect>` elements, the reference point is the top-left corner of the rectangle. In order to make the rectangle appear to slide along the path in the desired manner, we make two adjustments as follows:

1. The origin of the `<rect>` element (the **x** and **y** attributes) is defined as the point (-10, -50). Since the `<rect>` has a width of 20 and a height of 50, this has the effect of translating the

reference point to a position halfway along the bottom edge of the rectangle.

2. The modification detailed above relocates the rectangle's reference point, so that the element appears upright on the path. However, for a more realistic appearance, it may be desirable to rotate the object according to the slope of the path. We can achieve this by including a **rotate** attribute, with a value of **"auto"**. The effect of this can be seen in the images in Figure 6.42.

Figure 6.42
Using
<animateMotion>

```
<path d="M 20 200 C 50 00 300 400 380 150"
      style="fill:none; stroke: red; stroke-width: 2" />

<rect x="-10" y="-50" width="20" height="50"
      style="stroke:black; stroke-width:2; fill:none">
    <animateMotion dur="5s"
             path="M 20 200 C 50 300 300 400 380 150"
                   repeatCount="indefinite"
                   rotate="auto" />
</rect>
```

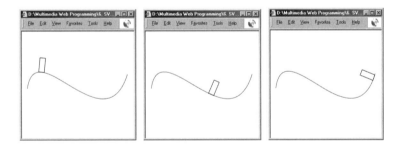

6.8.5 Using animateColor

The **<animateColor>** element allows us to modify the colour of a **stroke** or **fill** over time. Figure 6.43 illustrates an example where a **<text>** element is presented on top of a **<rect>**. A collection of **<animateColor>** elements is used to animate the **fill** property of the **<rect>**, and the **stroke** and **fill** properties of the **<text>**. The colours and period of each animation are different, thereby creating a wide range of effects, as demonstrated by the images below.

Figure 6.43
Using
`<animateColor>`

```
<rect x="0" y="0" width="400" height="400">
    <animateColor
        attributeName="fill"
        values="cyan; salmon; green; cyan"
        dur="10s" repeatCount="indefinite" />
</rect>

<text x="10" y="100"
    style="font-family:verdana; font-size:72;
        stroke-width:3">
    Animating

    <animateColor
        attributeName="fill" values="red; green; red"
        dur="3s" repeatCount="indefinite" />
    <animateColor
        attributeName="stroke"
        values="blue; yellow; blue"
        dur="6s" repeatCount="indefinite" />
</text>
```

The `<animateColor>` element interpolates between the colours specified in the values attribute. Cyclical animations are created by ensuring that the first and last colours in the values list are identical. Hence, the `fill` property of the `<rect>` element is interpolated from cyan to salmon; then from salmon to green; and finally from green back to cyan —over a 10-second period. Where only 2 colours are involved, and cyclical animation is not required, then `to` and `from` attributes can be specified instead of a `values` list. Hence the element

```
<animateColour attributeName="fill"
                from="red" to="blue"
                dur="3s" />
```

would interpolate the `fill` attribute of the target element from red to blue over a 3-second period.

6.8.6 Using `animateTransform`

In Section 6.4.2, we introduced the transformations that can be applied to groups of SVG elements. We can animate these by the `<animateTransform>` element. Figure 6.44 presents an animated rotation, applied to a group consisting of a `<circle>`, a `<path>` and a `<text>` element.

Figure 6.44
Animated
Transformations

```
<g>
   <circle cx="200" cy="150" r="10"
           style="fill:black; stroke:none" />
   <path d="M 200 150 L 150 250 250 250 Z"
         style="stroke:red; stroke-width:3; fill:none" />
   <text x="200" y="280"
         style="font-family:verdana; font-size:24;
                stroke:none; fill:blue;
                text-anchor:middle">Triangle
   </text>

   <animateTransform attributeName="transform"
                     type="rotate"
                     from="0 200 150" to="360 200 150"
                     dur="10s" repeatCount="indefinite" />
</g>
```

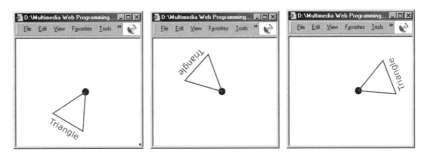

The attributes of the `<animateTransform>` are familiar from previous examples, but the `from` and `to` attributes require further explanation in this case.

The `from` and `to` elements are each specified by three numbers. The first value represents an angle in degrees, while the second and

213

third represent the x and y coordinates of the centre of the rotation. The example of Figure 6.45 continuously rotates the group of elements from 0° to 360° (i.e. a complete rotation), around the point (200, 150) —the centre of the `<circle>` element.

SUMMARY

- SVG provides a powerful environment for the specification of interactive graphical content on web pages.
- SVG is expressed in XML.
- In order to display SVG components, an SVG viewer is required.
- The `<svg>` container element describes the canvas on which the graphical elements are rendered.
- SVG supports a full range of basic shapes.
- The text capabilities of SVG are limited. Each string must be absolutely positioned, with no facility for automatic wraparound.
- SVG elements can be grouped so that transformations may be applied.
- SVG supports code reuse.
- A range of gradients, user-defined patters, filters and lighting models can be used to create complex graphical effects.
- SVG supports JavaScript for creating interactive, event-driven applications.
- A wide selection of animation elements allows us to specify complex sequences.

FURTHER INFORMATION

http://www.w3.org/Graphics/SVG/
The home of SVG on the web – the WWW Consortium.

http://www.svgelves.com
The SVG Developer Community on the web.

http://www.learnsvg.com

The website of the textbook – features sample chapter extracts.

http://wwws.sun.com/software/xml/developers/svg/
SVG Graphics – An Executive Summary, from Sun Microsystems.
Includes examples.

http://www.topxml.com/svg/default.asp
Explore the relationship between SVG and XML.

http://www.svgtutorial.com
Website of the (German) book. Includes links to interactive
examples.

http://www.adobe.com/svg/
Download the SVG viewer, and visit the tutorials and
demonstrations.

http://eluzions.com/Pictures/Illusions/Dynamic/
A set of optical illusions written in SVG.

http://www.wdvl.com/Authoring/Languages/XML/SVG/
Web Developer's Virtual Library – SVG Resources. Frequently
updated links to tutorials and demonstrations.

EXERCISES

1. Implement each of the code examples provided in the text. Try modifying various parameters and attributes in each example until you are comfortable with their operation.

2. Use the basic SVG elements to create a house object as illustrated below. Complete the drawing with a range of appropriate colours and fills.

3. Add event handling to the house constructed in problem 2 by simulating a light being turned on and off in a room. When the mouse is moved over a window, its colour should be set to yellow (the light is turned "on"). When the mouse is moved off the window again, it reverts to its initial state.

4. Add animation to the house constructed in problem 2 as follows. Initially the house should be invisible. Then, the house should fade into view over a period of 3 seconds. At the end of this period, the lights in the windows come on (as above) at a rate of 1 window each second. When all windows are on, the entire animation process is reversed —i.e. the lights go off in reverse order, and the house fades into the background. Additionally, during the entire 14 second period of the animation a white "moon" object should follow an arc trajectory above the house — starting on the left and finishing on the right.

5. A number of people were asked to select their favourite flavour of soup and responded as follows: Chicken 27%, Tomato 16%, Vegetable 20%, Beef 9%, Mushroom 28%. Construct an animated SVG presentation that presents this information as a series of histograms. Experiment with different fills, gradients and patterns for the histograms.

6. Use a range of SVG elements and animation techniques to create a "splash" introduction screen for a website. When the animation is complete, the user should be invited to click on some element to gain admittance to the main website.

7. Combine the techniques introduced in this chapter to produce a website entirely constructed in SVG.

8. Produce an animated menu as a SVG component that can be easily applied to any web page. The menu should consist of a permanently visible title bar, where each entry reveals a drop-down list of options when the mouse cursor passes over it. Clicking on an option links the user to the appropriate destination, while moving the mouse off the menu causes the list of options to be hidden again.

Synchronised Multimedia Integration Language

CHAPTER OBJECTIVES

In this chapter, we address the following key questions.

- What is the Synchronised Multimedia Integration Language (SMIL)?
- What is HTML+TIME?
- What is the relationship between SMIL/HTML+TIME and SVG?
- How do we specify timed elements in our web pages?
- How do we coordinate the appearance and disappearance of timed elements?
- What is a timeline and what types of timelines are available in SMIL?
- How do we specify event-driven animation in SMIL?
- How does SMIL handle embedded media objects?
- What structures are available for animating attributes of page elements?
- How can we model acceleration and deceleration in the animation of element attributes?
- What transitions are available to control the appearance and disappearance of page elements?

7.1 Introduction to SMIL and HTML+TIME

The Synchronised Multimedia Integration Language (SMIL) is an XML-based notation for the specification of media-rich presentations, including time-dependent elements and embedded multimedia content such as audio and video.

In this chapter, we focus on HTML+TIME, an implementation of SMIL for web browsers. HTML+TIME is supported by Microsoft Internet Explorer v5.5 and above, and uses SMIL structures to incorporate timing information into web pages. Using HTML+TIME, we can specify the time when elements should appear on a page, and the time at which they are removed. We can also animate our page elements using a range of structures similar to those available in SVG.

7.2 Timed Page Elements

7.2.1 A Framework for Timed Pages

HTML+TIME pages comprise standard HTML content, enhanced in two ways:

1. The inclusion of "new" HTML+TIME elements.
2. The application of timed attributes to native HTML elements.

In order to use the "new" HTML+TIME elements, we need to declare the XML *namespace* with whatever prefix we wish to use for our timed elements. In order to emphasise the close relationship between HTML+TIME and SMIL, we choose to use the prefix "smil". The namespace is thus declared with the tag

```
<html xmlns:smil="urn:schemas-microsoft-com:time">
```

We now need to import the Microsoft **time2** behaviour into the declared namespace by including the following command in the **<head>** of the document.

```
<?import namespace="smil"
         implementation="#default#time2">
```

In order to specify timed attributes to "normal" HTML elements, we need to declare the Microsoft **time2** behaviour as a style class. We then apply this class to any element to which we want to apply time control. Again, we choose the label "**smil**" for the style class, as follows.

```
<style>
    .smil { behavior: url(#default#time2); }
</style>
```

Figure 7.1 illustrates a skeleton for a page that includes HTML+TIME content. This skeleton will form the basis for all of the examples presented in this chapter.

Figure 7.1
Structure of a Timed
HTML Document

```
<html xmlns:smil="urn:schemas-microsoft-com:time">

<head>
    <?import namespace="smil"
             implementation="#default#time2">

    <style>
        .smil { behavior: url(#default#time2); }
    </style>
</head>

<body>

  <!-- Page elements go here
       Timed page elements reference
       the ".smil" class definition
    -->

</body>

</html>
```

7.2.2 Simple Timed Elements

The simplest way to apply *time* to page content is to specify when the element is to appear, and for how long it is to remain visible.

219

Figure 7.2 presents an example where five elements are manipulated as follows.

1. An `<h2>` element with no time information specified is displayed permanently.

2. An `<h3>` element appears 1 second after the page has loaded, and remains visible for a period of 4 seconds.

3. A `<p>` element appears 2 seconds after the page has loaded, and remains visible for a period of 3 seconds. The `<p>` is therefore removed at the same time as the `<h3>`.

4. A second `<h3>` element appears 5 seconds after the page has loaded (i.e. at the same time as the previous `<h3>` is removed). This element remains visible until a time 9 seconds after the page has loaded (i.e. the element remains visible for a period of 4 seconds).

5. A second `<p>` element appears 6 seconds after the page has loaded. This element is removed 9 seconds after page load.

Figure 7.2
Simple Timed Elements

```
<h2>Simple timed Elements</h2>

<h3 class="smil" begin="1" dur="4">
    1. The BEGIN attribute</h3>
<p class="smil" begin="2" dur="3">
    The BEGIN attribute determines the time at
    which the element is displayed.
    </p>

<h3 class="smil" begin="5" end="9">
    2. The DUR attribute</h3>
<p class="smil" begin="6" end="9">
    The DUR attribute determines the duration
    during which the element remains active.
    </p>
```

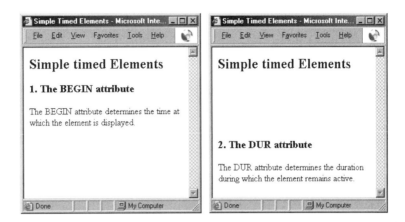

The *time* information is applied in the style attributes `begin`, `dur` (duration) and `end`. These (and other) attributes are made available by applying the style class `smil` to the element (or whatever name we choose to call the class that contains the **time2** behaviour). For example, the *time* style attributes applied to the first `<h3>` element

```
begin="1" dur="4"
```

specify that the element is to appear 1 second after the page loads, and is to remain visible for a period of 4 seconds.

Likewise, the *time* style attributes applied to the second `<h3>` element

```
begin="5" end="9"
```

specify that the element is to appear 5 seconds after the page loads, and disappear 9 seconds after the page loads (i.e. it remains visible for a period of 4 seconds).

Where no time information is specified (e.g. the `<h2>` element in Figure 7.2) then the element is displayed for the entire life of the page. If we have a `begin` element, but no `dur` or `end`, then the element displays at the appointed time, and remains visible for the remainder of the life of the page.

HTML+TIME is constructed around the notion of timelines, where a timeline is a series of timed events that describe the behaviour and appearance of the element. The timeline of the first `<h2>` element can be described as

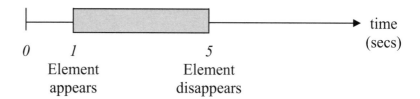

0   1   5   time
                                                                     (secs)
    Element   Element
    appears   disappears

while combining all elements gives a timeline for the presentation as follows.

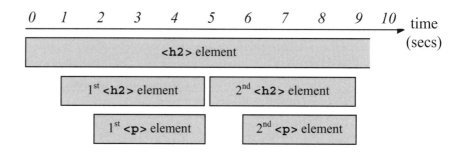

The default metric for the timed attributes is *seconds elapsed after the page load event.* However, we can also express these values in ms (milliseconds), m (minutes), h (hours) and assorted combinations of these as follows.

2:34:56	2 hours 34 minutes 56 seconds
2:34	2 minutes 34 seconds
2:34:00	2 hours 34 minutes
56.78	56 seconds 78 milliseconds
34:56.78	34 minutes 56 seconds 78 milliseconds

In addition to specifying time as relative to the page load event, we can also express a "real world" time by using the **wallclock()** function. This enables us to express a date in the form yyyy-mm-dd and a time in the form hh:mm:ss, with the date and time values separated by a "**T**". For example, the attribute assignment

```
begin="wallclock(2005-12-25T15:15:00)"
```

will render the target element active at 3:15 p.m. on the 25th of December, 2005.

7.2.3   Element-relative Timing

HTML+TIME supports *relative element timing*, where we can specify the beginning and end of element timelines relative to the timelines of other elements. For example if we require a pair of elements to appear at the same time, we might specify

```
<p class="smil" id="first" begin="2">
   Hello</p>

<p class="smil id="second"
   begin="first.begin">
   World</p>
```

which explicitly sets the time at which the first element becomes active, and ties the second element to begin at the same time. In this way, if we want to change the time at which the pair of elements become active, then we only have to change the `begin` attribute of the first element. The `begin` of the second will follow automatically.

We can also specify `begin` and `end` as an offset from a timeline. For example, if we wanted the element *second* to end 3 seconds after the element *first*, we might specify

```
<p class="smil" id="second"
   end="first.end+3">
   World</p>
```

Figure 7.3 presents the simple timed example of Figure 7.2, with the time attributes expressed as relative offset quantities.

223

Figure 7.3
Element-Relative
Timing

```
<h2>Simple timed Elements</h2>

<h3 class="smil" id="first" begin="1" dur="4">
    1. The BEGIN attribute</h3>
<p class="smil" begin="first.begin+1" end="first.end">
    The BEGIN attribute determines the time
    at which the element is displayed.</p>

<h3 class="smil" id="second" begin="first.end" dur="4">
    2. The DUR attribute</h3>
<p class="smil" begin="second.begin+1" end="second.end">
    The DUR attribute determines the
    duration during which the element remains active.</p>
```

7.2.4 Other Simple Time Properties

7.2.4.1 Multiple `begin` Attributes

We can specify multiple **begin** times for an element by specifying them as a semicolon-separated list. For example, the following code will cause a paragraph to blink on and off four times, at 2-second intervals.

```
<p class="smil" begin="0; 4; 8; 10" dur="2">
```

By this definition, the paragraph will appear when the page loads (time=0), disappear after 2 seconds (when the **dur** expires), reappear after 4 seconds, disappear after 6 seconds… and so on until the final appearance and disappearance at 10 and 12 seconds.

7.2.4.2 The `repeatCount` and `repeatDur` Attributes

The **repeatCount** attribute specifies the number of times an element should repeat. For example, the "multiple begin" example above could be expressed as

```
<p class="smil" begin="0" dur="2"
    repeatCount="4">
```

Fractional values for `repeatCount` are also possible, and denote that the final iteration is only partially completed. For example, the specification

```
<p class="smil" begin="0" dur="2"
    repeatCount="3.25">
```

results in the paragraph element being displayed for 3 full periods of 2 seconds, and a final period of 0.5 seconds (0.25 of the full 2 second period).

The `repeatDur` attribute is similar to `repeatCount`, except that the repetition is expressed as a time quantity. Hence, the code

```
<p class="smil" begin="0" dur="2"
    repeatDur="7.5">
```

specifies that the element will repeat for a total duration of 7.5 seconds —equivalent to a `repeatCount` of 3.75.

7.2.5 The `timeAction` Attribute

When we examine the example of Figure 7.2, we can see that timed elements continue to occupy an area on the page, even when they are inactive. This is evidenced by the rightmost image of Figure 7.2, where the first `<h3>` and `<p>` elements are rendered "below" the first, even though the previously displayed elements (shown on the leftmost image) have ceased to be active and are therefore not presented.

We can override this default behaviour by setting the `timeAction` attribute, which determines the action to be taken when a timed page element is inactive. The `timeAction` attribute takes one of four values as follows.

`visibility`	The default state. The element is visible when active, and invisible when inactive. When invisible, the element continues to occupy space on the page, resulting in the effect shown in Figure 7.2.

display	The element is visible when active, and invisible when inactive. However, when inactive, the element ceases to occupy any space on the page —causing other element to re-flow accordingly.
style	The element is displayed with the inline style when the element is active, and is displayed without the inline style when the element is inactive.
class:*classname*	The specified class name(s) is/are applied to the element when the element is active. The element is displayed without the inline style(s) when it is inactive.

Figure 7.4 demonstrates the effect of setting `timeAction=display` by implementing a slideshow-like application, where the automatic repositioning when elements expire results in each `<h3>` and `<p>` pair occupying the position of the previous pair.

Figure 7.4
Creating a Simple Slideshow

```
<h2>Simple timed Elements</h2>

<h3 class="smil" begin="1" dur="4" timeAction="display">
    1. The <em>begin</em> attribute</h3>
<p class="smil" begin="2" dur="3" timeAction="display">
    The <em>begin</em> attribute determines the time at
    which the element is displayed.
    </p>
```

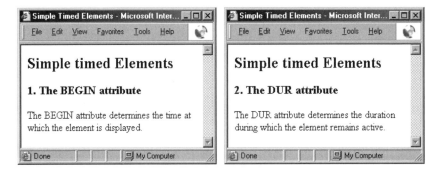

226

Figure 7.5 demonstrates the effect of setting
`timeAction=style`, where the elements are enclosed in a **`<span>`**
tag that applies a text colour to the entire collection of elements. In
addition, each element has an inline style definition that changes the
colour of the element, and is applied only when the element is active.
The effect is illustrated in Figure 7.5, where elements appear to be
highlighted during the active period of each element. The images
represent the state of the presentation at 0 seconds (after page load),
2 seconds and 5 seconds.

Figure 7.5
Timed Application of
Style Attributes

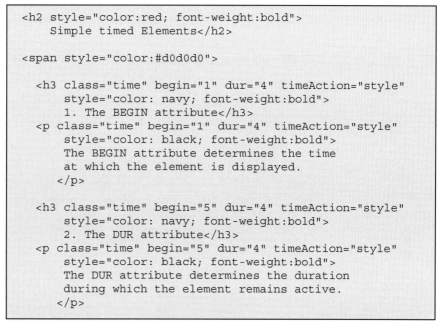

```
<h2 style="color:red; font-weight:bold">
    Simple timed Elements</h2>

<span style="color:#d0d0d0">

  <h3 class="time" begin="1" dur="4" timeAction="style"
      style="color: navy; font-weight:bold">
      1. The BEGIN attribute</h3>
  <p class="time" begin="1" dur="4" timeAction="style"
      style="color: black; font-weight:bold">
      The BEGIN attribute determines the time
      at which the element is displayed.
      </p>

  <h3 class="time" begin="5" dur="4" timeAction="style"
      style="color: navy; font-weight:bold">
      2. The DUR attribute</h3>
  <p class="time" begin="5" dur="4" timeAction="style"
      style="color: black; font-weight:bold">
      The DUR attribute determines the duration
      during which the element remains active.
      </p>
```

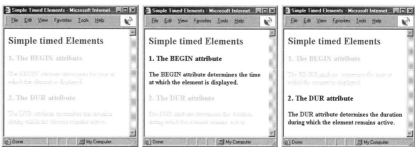

7.3 Interactivity

7.3.1 Event-Driven Interaction

Previous examples have illustrated timing interdependence between page elements. It is also possible to implement user interaction by having elements respond to mouse events. Figure 7.6 further develops the "slideshow" example of Figure 7.5, by moving from slide to slide only when the user clicks on a **<button>** object.

In Figure 7.6, each **<h3>** and **<p>** element pair is augmented by a **<button>** object, which is timed to become active 2 seconds after the elements are displayed. The click event of the button is the trigger to remove the **<h3>** and **<p>**, as well as the **<button>**. Because the second **<h3>** and **<p>** pair is chained to the end event of the first **<h3>**, the user can use the button to navigate from screen to screen.

Figure 7.6
Mouse-Driven
Interaction

```
<h2>Mouse-Driven Timing</h2>

<h3 class="smil" id="first" begin="1"
    end="continue1.click"  timeAction="display">
    1. The BEGIN attribute</h3>
<p class="smil" begin="first.begin+1"
   end="continue1.click" timeAction="display">
   The BEGIN attribute determines the time
   at which the element is displayed.</p>

<button class="smil" id="continue1" timeAction="display"
        begin="first.begin+2" end="continue1.click">
        Click here to continue</button>

<h3 class="smil" id="second" begin="first.end"
    end="continue2.click" timeAction="display">
    2. The DUR attribute</h3>
<p class="smil" begin="second.begin+1"
   end="continue2.click" timeAction="display">
   The DUR attribute determines the duration
   during which the element remains active.</p>

<button class="smil" id="continue2" timeAction="display"
        begin="second.begin+2" end="continue2.click">
        Click here to continue</button>
```

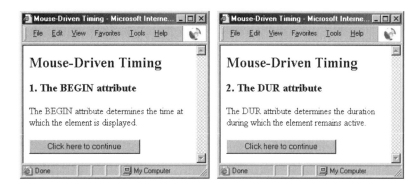

Timed HTML elements also support the **beginElement()** method, which can be used by other elements to remotely invoke the element in response to some event.

This is demonstrated by Figure 7.7, which implements a countdown application by defining the five stages of the countdown as chained paragraph elements, each with a duration of 1 second, and each starting 1 second after its predecessor.

The application also includes a **<button>** element, which, when pressed, enables the user to restart the countdown by invoking the first paragraph element in the chain. In addition, we need to specify **end="reset.click"** for each of the stages of the countdown so that the currently displayed paragraph is removed immediately the button is clicked.

Figure 7.7
External Control of
Timed Elements

```
<p id="start" class="smil" begin="0" dur="1"
   timeAction="display">
      Countdown</p>
<p class="smil" begin="start.end" dur="1"
             end="reset.click" timeAction="display">
      Three....</p>
<p class="smil" begin="start.end+1" dur="1"
   end="reset.click" timeAction="display">
      Two....</p>
<p class="smil" begin="start.end+2" dur="1"
   end="reset.click" timeAction="display">
      One....</p>
<p class="smil" begin="start.end+3" end="reset.click"
   timeAction="display">
      Lift Off!!!!</p>

<button id="reset" onclick="start.beginElement()">
      Click to reset counter
</button>
```

7.4   Timeline Containers

7.4.1   What is a Timeline Container?

HTML+TIME is constructed around the notion of **timelines**, which enable us to specify and control the temporal relationship between page elements. This relationship may be *static*, with each element having well-defined explicit properties **begin** and **dur/end**; or it may be *event-based*, with synchronisation expressed in terms of element activity.

Timeline containers provide a mechanism by which we can combine different synchronisation models in a single document. Three timeline containers are available:

1. **sequential timelines**, defining elements which run in sequence;

2. **parallel timelines**, where multiple elements can be active at the same time;

3. **exclusive timelines**, where elements can run in any order, but only one at a time.

7.4.2   The `<smil:seq>` Timeline Container

The `<smil:seq>` element allows us to specify a collection of page elements which become active in series, with no more than one element active at a time. The first element in the sequence begins with the begin value of the `<smil:seq>` container, with subsequent elements becoming active immediately upon the expiry of their predecessor.

Figure 7.8 presents a simple slideshow application implemented with the **<smil:seq>** container.

Figure 7.8
*The **<smil:seq>***
Timeline Container

```
<head>
 <style>
    .smil   { behavior: url(#default#time2) }

    .slide { width:300; height:200;
             font-family:verdana; font-size:36pt;
             font-weight:bold;
             text-align:center; color:white }
 </style>
 <?import namespace="smil" implementation="#default#time2">
</head>

<body>
  <smil:seq begin="0">
     <div class="smil slide" style="background-color:red"
         dur="3">
             Slide 1</div>
     <div class="smil slide"
         style="background-color:orange" dur="3">
             Slide 2</div>
     <div class="smil slide"
         style="background-color:yellow" dur="3">
             Slide 3</div>
  </smil:seq>
</body>
```

When using the **<smil:seq>** container, it is important to set the **dur** or **end** property of each element, as the next element cannot display until the current one has expired. There is no need to set the **begin** property of an element; but if it is used, then it is expressed as an offset from the time at which the element would naturally begin. For example, the code

```
<smil:seq begin="0">
   <div class="smil" dur="3">
        First element</div>
   <div class="smil" start="1" dur="3">
        Second element</div>
</smil:seq>
```

would cause the first element to begin at time=0 (the start time of the sequence), and the second element to begin at time=4 (1 second after the time at which the element would normally become active).

7.4.3   The `<smil:par>` Timeline Container

The `<smil:par>` container provides a framework in which multiple elements can be active at the same time. The **begin** and **end** of an element in a `<smil:par>` container are expressed relative to the **begin** time for the container. The `<body>` of a HTML+TIME document is an implicit `<smil:par>` container.

Figure 7.9
The `<smil:par>`
Timeline Container

```
<head>
   <style>
     .smil  { behavior: url(#default#time2) }
     .slideHead {
             font-family:verdana; font-size:24pt;
             font-weight:bold;
             text-align:center; color:navy }
     .slideText {
             font-family:verdana; font-size:14pt;
             font-weight:bold;
             text-align:center; color:black }
   </style>
   <?import namespace="smil"
         implementation="#default#time2">
</head>

<body>
   <smil:par begin="0">
     <p class="smil slideHead" begin="0">
        &lt;smil:par&gt;</p>
     <p class="smil slideText" begin="1">
        Presentation elements<br>that overlap in time</p>
     <p class="smil slideText" begin="2">
        Timing expressed relative to<br>
        the start of the timeline</p>
   </smil:par>
</body>
```

Figure 7.9 illustrates the contents of a slide as a `<smil:par>` container, where components of the slide are added over the lifetime of the container. This example contains three paragraph elements, which are made active at 0, 1 and 2 seconds respectively. Since none of the paragraphs has a **dur** or **end** attribute specified, they remain visible until the expiry of the timeline container.

7.4.4 The `<smil:excl>` Timeline Container

The `<smil:excl>` container provides a framework for a group of related elements, where only one of the group can be active at a time. If a member of the group becomes active while another member is already being presented, then the first element is removed so that the new element can begin.

The `<smil:excl>` container is often used in interactive presentations, where the user selects the element to be displayed from a menu. Figure 7.10 illustrates such a situation, where the user chooses which of three slides is to be displayed by clicking on the appropriate button.

Figure 7.10
The `<smil:excl>`
Timeline Container

```
<head>
  <style>
    .smil { behavior: url(#default#time2) }
    .slide {width:300; height:200;
            font-family:verdana; font-size:36pt;
            font-weight:bold;
            text-align:center; color:white }
  </style>
  <?import namespace="smil"
          implementation="#default#time2">
</head>

<body>
  <smil:excl>
    <div id="s1" class="smil slide" timeAction="display"
         style="background-color:red" begin="0">
      Slide 1</div>
    <div id="s2" class="smil slide" timeAction="display"
         style="background-color:orange" >
      Slide 2</div>
    <div id="s3" class="smil slide" timeAction="display"
         style="background-color:yellow">
      Slide 3</div>
  </smil:excl>

  <table width="300">
    <tr align="center">
      <td><button onclick="s1.beginElement()">
          Slide 1</button></td>
      <td><button onclick="s2.beginElement()">
          Slide 2</button></td>
      <td><button onclick="s3.beginElement()">
          Slide 3</button></td>
    </tr>
  </table>
</body>
```

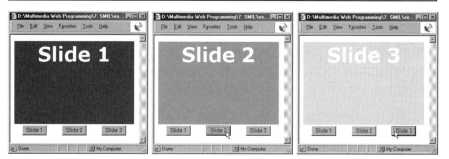

Figure 7.10 specifies a `<smil:excl>` container, which holds
definitions of three slide objects, each represented as a `<div>`

element. Only the first slide has a **begin** time set, hence this is the slide first displayed when the page loads.

The set of **<button>** objects provide a means for the user to select which slide is to be displayed. When a button is clicked, the **beginElement()** method causes the requested slide to become active, replacing the currently displayed object.

7.4.5 Multiple Timeline Containers

Combining timeline containers enables us to create complex synchronised presentations. Figure 7.11 uses the sequential, parallel and exclusive timelines previously discussed to create an application where the user chooses which of a collection of slideshow presentations is to be displayed.

The presentations are specified as the children of a **<smil:excl>** container, with the presentation to be displayed selected from a set of buttons as described in Figure 7.10. Each presentation is then represented as a series of individual slides, gathered together in a **<smil:seq>** container —giving a framework for the application as described below.

```
<smil:excl>
   <smil:seq>
        <!-- series of slides for
             the first presentation -->
   </smil:seq>

   <smil:seq>
        <!-- series of slides for
             the second presentation -->
   </smil:seq>
</smil:excl>
```

We now create each slide as a **<smil:par>** container, with the slide components appearing and disappearing at different times as required. The **dur** property of the **<smil:par>** container specifies the total time for which the slide is displayed, with each element of the slide becoming active within that period according to its **begin** attribute. CSS attributes are applied to the slide container and to the individual elements to implement a consistent presentation style across slides and slideshows.

Figure 7.11 presents the finished slideshow application. When the page loads, the first presentation is displayed by default (`begin="0"`). This presentation will loop (`repeatCount="indefinite"`), until another is selected by clicking on the appropriate button.

Figure 7.11
Multiple Timeline
Containers

```
<head>
    <style>
        .smil { behavior: url(#default#time2) }
        .slide {width:300; height:200 }
        .slideHead { font-family:verdana; font-size:24pt;
                    font-weight:bold; text-align:center;
                    color:navy }
        .slideText { font-family:verdana; font-size:12pt;
                    font-weight:bold; text-align:center;
                    color:white }
    </style>
    <?import namespace="smil"
            implementation="#default#time2">
</head>

<body>

<smil:excl>
  <smil:seq id="presentation1"
          repeatCount="indefinite" begin="0">
    <smil:par class="smil slide"
            style="background-color:red"
            dur="4" timeAction="display">
        <p class="smil slideHead" begin="0">
        &lt;smil:par&gt;</p>
        <p class="smil slideText" begin="1">
        Presentation elements<br>
        that overlap in time</p>
        <p class="smil slideText" begin="2">
        Timing expressed relative to<br>
        the timeline start</p>
    </smil:par>
    <smil:par class="smil slide"
            style="background-color:orange"
            dur="4" timeAction="display">
        <p class="smil slideHead" begin="0">
        &lt;smil:seq&gt;</p>
        <p class="smil slideText" begin="1">
        Presentation elements<br>in sequence</p>
        <p class="smil slideText" begin="2">
        Timing relative to the start of<br>
        the previous element</p>
    </smil:par>
```

```
            <smil:par class="smil slide"
                style="background-color:yellow"
                    dur="4" timeAction="display">
                <p class="smil slideHead" begin="0">
                    &lt;smil:excl&gt;</p>
                <p class="smil slideText" begin="1">
                    One element displayed<br>at a time</p>
            </smil:par>
        </smil:seq>

        <smil:seq id="presentation2" repeatCount="indefinite">
            <!-- Definition of next presentation goes here -->
        </smil:seq>
    </smil:excl>

    <table width="300">
        <tr align="center">
            <td><button onclick="presentation1.beginElement()">
                    Presentation 1</button></td>
            <td><button onclick="presentation2.beginElement()">
                    Presentation 2</button></td>
        </tr>
    </table>
    </body>
```

7.5   Media Elements

7.5.1   Embedded Media

SMIL/HTML+TIME makes it easy to embed media objects in our presentations, and to schedule and synchronise those objects in the same way as for other content. The following media elements are available.

237

```
<smil:media>
<smil:video>
<smil:audio>
<smil:image>
<smil:animation>
<smil:ref>
```

All of these elements are functionally identical, but are provided to enable us to produce more easily understood code. For example, we might use `<smil:animation>` to present an animated gif, while playing a piece of background music with `<smil:audio>`. However, it would be equally correct to embed both elements using `<smil:media>`, or indeed any of the other media elements.

All media elements support the `begin`, `end`, `dur`, `repeatCount` and `repeatDur` properties introduced earlier. In addition, a `src` property is used to specify the media file to be embedded. For example, we might supply background music for a presentation by including the code

```
<smil:audio src="music.mp3" begin="0"
            repeatCount="indefinite" />
```

to denote that the audio file begins to play as soon as the page loads, and repeats for as long as the page is viewed.

Continuous media elements such as audio, video and animation also support the properties `clipBegin` and `clipEnd`, which enable us to specify a subset of the media for presentation. For example, we might choose only to play the second minute of the audio file (the portion between 60 seconds and 120 seconds) of the previous example by specifying

```
<smil:audio src="music.mp3" begin="0"
        repeatCount="indefinite"
        clipBegin="60" clipEnd="120" />
```

Figure 7.12 demonstrates an mpeg video clip embedded into a HTML+TIME presentation with the `<smil:media>` element. Playback of the video is controlled by a set of four buttons that invoke methods to *begin*, *pause*, *resume* (after pause) or *end* playback. Note how we do not have to specify the media player —

HTML+TIME will select the appropriate player based on the type of file supplied in the `src` attribute. Also, note that the player has no visual appearance other then the actual video clip. Any interface to the player must be provided by the HTML+TIME presentation.

Figure 7.12
Embedded Media

```
<smil:media id="myMedia"
            src="polarBear.mpeg"
            begin="indefinite"/>
<br>

<button onclick="myMedia.beginElement()">
      Start</button>
<button onclick="myMedia.pauseElement()">
      Pause</button>
<button onclick="myMedia.resumeElement()">
      Resume</button>
<button onclick="myMedia.endElement()">
      Stop</button>
```

7.5.2   Using the Slider Behaviour

In order to build an interface to our simple media player of Figure 7.12, we require some means by which we can specify random access to any location within the continuous media element. In this example, we make use of the *Microsoft Slider Behaviour*.

Element Behaviours provide us with a way of defining new components that can then be used in web applications. Once attached to a page (through the `<style>` element), they can be used as native HTML elements. Figure 7.13 illustrates the specification and visual appearance of the *slider* behaviour, which is available for download from http://msdn.microsoft.com.

Figure 7.13
The Slider Behaviour

```
<html xmlns:slide>
<head>
   <style>
      @media all
         { slide\:slider behavior:url(slider.htc) }
   </style>
</head>

<body>
   <slide:slider />
</body>

</html>
```

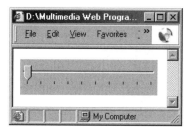

The slider is an input device that allows us to specify a position within a predefined range. A set of attributes enables us to customise the slider to our own application by defining the limits of the range, the number and style of the ticks that mark positions along the range, and the physical dimension of the slider.

We will use the slider behaviour in our media player to provide feedback on the current position within the continuous media element, as well as providing a means of providing direct access to any position within the element.

7.5.3 Building the Basic Media Player

The media player application consists of a `<smil:media>` element which embeds the media item; a slider behaviour to reflect the current position within the media item; and a set of buttons to enable the user to start, stop, pause and resume playback. The slider is customised according to the following attributes:

```
min=0 max=100
```
A slider property that enables us to customise the range. In this case, the slider will report the position within the media element as a percentage of the total duration of the media.

```
tickNumber:101
```
A slider style property that determines the number of different slider positions. Here, we choose to provide a different position for each of the possible slider values in the range 0-100.

```
sl-tick-style:none
```
A slider style property that determines the way in which the ticks are presented on the slider. Here, we choose not to display the ticks.

When the page is loaded, the load event invokes a JavaScript function **setUpTimer()**, which sets up an interrupt-driven call to the function **updateTimes()**. This will result in **updateTimes** being executed once every second (1000 milliseconds).

The purpose of **updateTimes** is to move the slider so that it accurately reflects the current location within the media element. We do this by obtaining the current position within the media item (**myMedia.currTimeState.simpleTime**) and converting it to a percentage of the total duration (**myMedia.mediaDur**). The result is then applied to the **value** attribute of the slider element.

In this example, we also use HTML+TIME behaviour to ensure that only one of the *pause* or *resume* buttons is presented at a time. When the application loads, the *pause* button is presented and the *resume* button is hidden. If the *pause* button is pressed, then it is hidden and the *resume* button made available. Once the presentation has been resumed, then the *pause* button once again appears.

This is implemented by specifying the **begin** and **end** attributes of the buttons in terms of button activity. Hence for the *pause* button, we have

```
begin="0; resumeButton.click"
end="pauseButton.click"
```

and for the *resume* button

```
begin="pauseButton.end"
end="resumeButton.click"
```

This denotes that the *pause* button is displayed when the page is first loaded (`time=0`) and remains present until that button is clicked. The removal of the *pause* button then triggers the presentation of the *resume* button, which remains in place until it is subsequently clicked. The removal of the *resume* button then causes the *pause* button to be presented once more.

    The basic media player application is presented in Figure 7.14. Note that the `<head>` tag must include **XML namespace** references for both the slider and HTML+TIME behaviours.

Figure 7.14
A Basic Media Player

```
<head>
  <style>
    .smil { behavior: url(#default#time2) }
    @media all {
        control\:slider { behavior:url(slider.htc) }
    }
  </style>

  <?import namespace="smil"
          implementation="#default#time2">

  <script language="JavaScript">
     function setUpTimer() {
       window.setInterval(updateTimes,1000);
     }

     function updateTimes() {
       mySlider.value=
          Math.round((myMedia.currTimeState.simpleTime/
               myMedia.mediaDur)*100);
     }
  </script>
</head>

<body onLoad="setUpTimer()">

   <smil:media id="myMedia" src="movie.mpeg"
               begin="indefinite" /><br>

   <control:slider id="mySlider" MIN="0" MAX="100"
               style="sl--tick-style:none;
                      height:30; tickNumber:101" /><br>
```

```
<table width="200">
<tr>
  <td width="33%" align="center">
    <button onclick="myMedia.beginElement()">
            Start</button></td>
  <td width="33%" align="center">
    <button class="smil" id="pauseButton"
            timeAction="display"
            begin="0; resumeButton.click"
            end="pauseButton.click"
            onclick="myMedia.pauseElement()">
        Pause</button>
    <button class="smil" id="resumeButton"
            timeAction="display"
            begin="pauseButton.end"
            end="resumeButton.click"
            onclick="myMedia.resumeElement()">
        Resume</button></td>
  <td width="33%" align="center">
    <button onclick="myMedia.endElement()"
            width="70">
        Stop</button></td></tr>
</table>

</body>
</html>
```

7.5.4   Adding the Seek Functionality

We complete the simple media player application by providing the ability to jump directly to any point in the media element by dragging the slider to the required location. This is implemented by using the media seek tools available in HTML+TIME and is

243

illustrated in Figure 7.15, with the newly added code presented in bold text.

Figure 7.15
Basic Media Player with Seek Functionality

```
...
<head>
<script language="JavaScript">
...
    function updateSlider() {
        if (mySlider.value!=
            Math.round((myMedia.currTimeState.simpleTime/
                         myMedia.mediaDur)*100))
            myMedia.seekActiveTime(mySlider.value*
                                     myMedia.mediaDur/100);
    }
</script>
</head>

<body>

...
<control:slider ID="mySlider" ...
     onchange="updateSlider()" />
...

</body>
</html>
```

We invoke seeking by monitoring the **onchange** event of the slider behaviour. However, we need to be certain that the slider has not changed due to the normal progression of the media, so the **updateSlider()** function first checks that the new position of the slider does not correspond to the expected position. If it is found that the position of the slider does not correspond to the current playback position of the media, then the **seekActiveTime** method is used to jump to the location in the media element that corresponds to the new value of the slider.

7.6 Specifying and Controlling Animation

7.6.1 Specifying Animation

Animation in SMIL/HTML+TIME is based around the manipulation of element attributes over time, specified by four animation elements.

7.6.1.1 The `<smil:animate>` Element

The `<smil:animate>` element is a general-purpose element which can be used to animate most properties of HTML elements. The `attributeName` property specifies the attribute to which the animation is to be applied. For example the code

```
<div id="myBox"
        style="width:100; height:100;
            background-color:blue" />
<smil:animate targetElement="myBox"
        attributeName="width"
            from="100" to="200" dur="5" />
```

will animate the `width` attribute of the element with `id` "myBox" from 100 pixels to 200 pixels, over a period of 5 seconds. Any attribute of the element can be animated in this way, as long as the attribute has first been explicitly set —hence the `width`, `height` and `background-color` properties are available for animation in this case.

7.6.1.2 The `<smil:animateMotion>` Element

The `<smil:animateMotion>` element can be used to animate the top and left properties of an element. As the element is specifically used for these properties, there is no need to use the `attributeName` attribute in this case. We could use `<smil:animateMotion>` to animate the position of the `myBox` element from the position (10, 50) to (100, 250) by the following code. Note again that we must set the properties through a CSS assignment before they become available for animation.

```
<div id="myBox"
      style="position:absolute; top:10;
             left:50" />
<smil:animate targetElement="myBox"
      to="100,250" dur="5" />
```

7.6.1.3   The `<smil:animateColor>` Element

The `<smil:animateColor>` element is used to change the colour of an object. We can specify the source and target colours using any of the usual notations. The following code animates the `background-color` property of the **myBox** element between blue and red.

```
<div id="myBox"
      style="width:100; height:100;
             background-color:blue" />
<smil:animateColor targetElement="myBox"
             to="red" dur="5" />
```

7.6.1.4   The `<smil:set>` Element

The `<smil:set>` element is used to assign a property directly to a value. For example, the following code changes the background colour of the **myBox** element from red to blue, taking effect 5 seconds after the page loads.

```
<div id="myBox"
      style="width:100; height:100;
             background-color:blue" />
<smil:set targetElement="myBox"
      attributeName="background-color"
      to="red" begin="5" />
```

246

It is possible to create more complex effects by combining animations, either within a `<smil:par>` container, or within the `<body>` of the document (which acts as an implied `<smil:par>`).

Figure 7.16 illustrates a box element that changes its position, shape and colour over a four-second period. Note the `fill="hold"` attribute that specifies that the final state of the target element is to be preserved when the animation is complete.

Figure 7.16
Combining
Animations

```
<div id="myBox" style="width:0; height:100;
                       background-color:blue;
                       position:absolute; top:0; left:0" />
<smil:animate targetElement="myBox" attributeName="width"
        from="0" to="100" begin="0" dur="4"
        fill="hold" />
<smil:animateMotion targetElement="myBox"
        from="0,0" to="500,250" begin="0" dur="4"
        fill="hold" />
<smil:animateColor targetElement="myBox"
        attributeName="background-color"
        values="blue; green; red; yellow"
        begin="0" dur="4" fill="hold" />
```

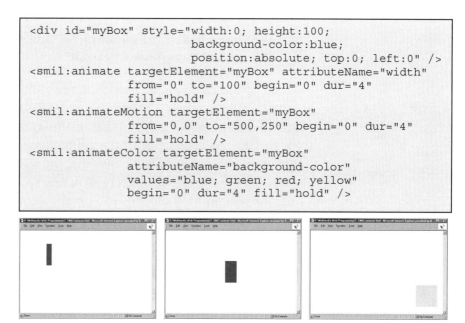

7.6.2 Calculating Intermediate Values

HTML+TIME provides a `calcMode` attribute, which allows us to specify how intermediate values for the animation are calculated. The default value for `calcMode` is "`linear`", which specifies that the target attribute should animate at a constant rate from the beginning value to the end value.

For example, the `<animate>` element

```
<animate targetElement="myBox"
    attributeName="width"
    from="100" to="500"
    calcMode="linear" dur="4" />
```

will cause the **width** of the target element to grow from 100 pixels to 500 pixels over a period of 4 seconds —at a constant rate of 100 pixels per second.

We can specify a series of rates to be used for the animation by replacing the **from** and **to** attributes with a single **values** attribute. This divides the animation into a number of stages, with each stage allocated an equal share of the duration.

For example, the element

```
<animate targetElement="myBox"
    attributeName="width"
    values="100; 400; 500"
    calcMode="linear" dur="4" />
```

identifies two stages to the animation: from 100 to 400, and from 400 to 500. As each stage of the animation is allocated an equal share of the duration, this dictates that the **width** will grow by 300 pixels over the first 2 seconds (150 pixels/second), and by 100 pixels over the remaining 2 seconds (50 pixels/second).

We can enhance this further by using the **keyTimes** attribute to allocate varying portions of the duration to different stages of the animation. The **keyTimes** attribute consists of a list of values in the range 0-1, where we have one value for each element in the values list. The entries in the **keyTimes** list represent the time (as a proportion of the duration) at which each entry in the **values** list is reached. For example, the element

```
<animate targetElement="myBox"
    attributeName="width"
    values="100; 400; 500"
    keyTimes="0; .25; 1"
    calcMode="linear" dur="4" />
```

describes the **width** property of the **myBox** element changing from 100 to 400 over a 1-second period (25% of the duration), followed by an animation from 400 to 500 over a 3-second period (the remaining 75% of the duration).

The **calcmode** attribute also supports **discrete** and **spline** interpolation of intermediate states. Setting **calcMode** to **discrete** causes the animation to jump directly from **begin** to **end** values, without interpolating through intermediate states. Spline interpolation is more complex, and is the subject of the following section.

7.6.2.1   Spline Interpolation

The **keySplines** attribute allows us to describe the rate of animation as a Bezier curve. The **keySplines** attribute is always used in conjunction with **keyTimes**, and views the values in **keyTimes** as the endpoints of the curve (through which the curve must pass), while **keySplines** holds the control points that influence the curve's shape.

Hence, to specify an animation function where the rate of change begins at a fast pace and gets slower as the animation proceeds, we might use the code

```
<animate targetElement="myBox"
    attributeName="width"
    values="100; 400" calcMode="spline"
    dur="4" keyTimes="0; 1"
    keySplines="0 .5 .5 1" />
```

This describes the rate of animation as a Bezier curve with endpoints (0, 0) and (1,1) and control points (0, .5) and (.5, 1). We can see this Bezier curve in Figure 7.17.

Figure 7.17
Deceleration
Function

We can interpret this curve by regarding the x-coordinate as time, and the y-coordinate as the attribute being animated. In this function, the y-coordinate changes rapidly at the beginning, and the rate of change slows as the curve proceeds.

Figure 7.18 presents other useful spline functions.

Figure 7.18
Other Spline
Functions

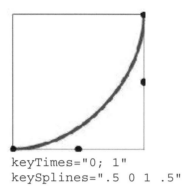

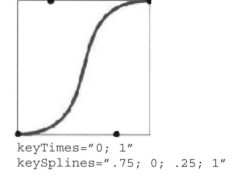

```
keyTimes="0; 1"
keySplines=".5 0 1 .5"
```

```
keyTimes="0; 1"
keySplines=".75; 0; .25; 1"
```

Rate increases as the
animation proceeds

Rate begins slowly, speeds up
then slows down again

7.7 Using Transitions

7.7.1 Specifying Transitions

Transitions are graphical effects such as *fades* and *wipes*, applied to the appearance or removal of an element on a page. They are particularly useful in applying a professional finish to presentations and slideshows.

Transitions can be applied to any element that is said to have *layout* —i.e. any element that occupies a well-defined region on the display area. The SMIL/HTML+TIME elements such as `<smil:media>` automatically have layout, others gain layout from having a dimension (e.g. width, height) or a position explicitly set.

HTML+TIME Transitions are applied through the `<smil:transitionfilter>` element. The attributes `<smil:transitionfilter>` determine the characteristics of the transition, such as the type of transition used, whether the element is being applied to the presentation or removed from it, and the time to be spent applying the transition.

Figure 7.19 demonstrates a *fade* `<transitionfilter>` applied to the presentation of a `<div>` element.

Figure 7.19
Specifying a
Transition

```
<div class="smil" id="myDiv" begin="2" dur="10"
    style=" position: absolute; left:10; top:10;
            height:200; width:200;
            background-color:blue">
    <h3 style="text-align:center; color:yellow">
        Transitions</h3>
    <p style="text-align:center; color:white">
        This element fades in</p>
</div>

<smil:transitionfilter targetElement="myDiv"
    begin="myDiv.begin" dur="2" mode="in" type="fade" />
```

The transition of Figure 7.19 is described by four attributes:

begin The time at which the transition is to be applied. In this case, the transition should begin at the same time as the element is activated.

dur The time spent applying the transition. Here, we specify that the transition should take 2 seconds from beginning to end.

mode determines whether the element to which the transition is applied is being presented or removed. In this case, the value **in** specifies that the transition is being applied to the presentation of an element.

type The identifier for the transition. Here we specify that a **fade** operation is to be applied.

251

It is possible to apply more than one
`<smil:transitionfilter>` to an element. Figure 7.20 presents
an object that fades in over 2 seconds, is displayed for 3 seconds, and
then fades out over a further 2 seconds.

Figure 7.20
Multiple Transitions

```
<div class="smil" id="myDiv" begin="2" dur="10"
     style=" position: absolute; left:10; top:10;
             height:200; width:200;
             background-color:blue">
    <h3 style="text-align:center; color:yellow">
        Transitions</h3>
    <p style="text-align:center; color:white">
        This element fades in and out</p>
</div>

<smil:transitionfilter targetElement="myDiv"
    begin="myDiv.begin" dur="2" mode="in" type="fade" />

<smil:transitionfilter targetElement="myDiv"
    begin="myDiv.end-2" dur="2" mode="out" type="fade" />
```

It is important to carefully coordinate the timing of the
`<smil:transitionfilter>` with the timing of the element to
which it is applied. With a transition in, it is generally desirable to
begin the transition with the **begin** of the target element; while with
a transition out, it is usual to coordinate the transition so that it
finishes just as the element is removed. If we deviate from this
schedule, the transitions will still take place (as long as they are
within the active period of the element), but the results may not be
visually pleasing.

7.7.2   Transition Types and Subtypes

HTML+TIME provides 15 variations of 12 different transitions, which are selected through the **type** and **subtype** attributes. The variations are presented in the following table.

Type	Subtype(s)
`barnDoorWipe`	`vertical, horizontal`
`barWipe`	`leftToRight, topToBottom`
`clockWipe`	`clockwiseTwelve`
`ellipseWipe`	`circle`
`Fade`	`crossFade`
`fanWipe`	`centerTop`
`irisWipe`	`rectangle, diamond`
`pushWipe`	`fromLeft`
`slideWipe`	`fromLeft`
`snakeWipe`	`topLeftHorizontal`
`spiralWipe`	`topLeftClockwise`
`starWipe`	`fivepoint`

If no **subtype** attribute is specified for a `<smil:transitionfilter>`, then the default **subtype** for that transition will be used, where the default is the first **subtype** listed. For example, we could specify the **rectangle** variant of the **irisWipe** by

```
<smil:transitionfilter
    targetElement="myDiv"
    begin="myDiv.begin" dur="2"
    mode="in"
    type="irisWipe"
    subtype="rectangle" />
```

or more succinctly (since **rectangle** is the default **subtype** of **irisWipe**) as

```
<smil:transitionfilter
    targetElement="myDiv"
    begin="myDiv.begin" dur="2"
    mode="in"
    type="irisWipe" />
```

253

The only exception to this rule is `type="starWipe"`, for which `subtype="fivePoint"` must be explicitly specified for the transition to take place. However, as a point of good practice, it is better to always explicitly state the desired subtype to be applied.

7.7.3   Combining Transitions

We can further increase the range of visual effects available by applying **multiple `<smil:transitionfilter>`** elements in parallel. Figure 7.21 illustrates the combination of a `fade` with a `clockWipe`. There is no restriction on the number and combination of transitions that can be simultaneously applied, although care must be taken to ensure that those applied are visually compatible.

Figure 7.21
Multiple
Simultaneous
Transitions

```
<div class="smil" id="myDiv" begin="2" dur="10"
    style=" position: absolute; left:10; top:10;
            height:200; width:200;
            background-color:blue">
    <h3 style="text-align:center; color:yellow">
        Transitions</h3>
    <p style="text-align:center; color:white">
        This element has multiple
        simultaneous transitions</p>
</div>

<smil:transitionfilter targetElement="myDiv"
    begin="myDiv.begin" dur="4" mode="in"
    type="fade" />

<smil:transitionfilter targetElement="myDiv"
    begin="myDiv.begin" dur="4" mode="in"
    type="clockwipe" />
```

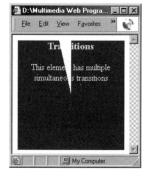

SUMMARY

- The Synchronised Multimedia Integration Language (SMIL) is an XML-based notation for the specification of interactive presentations including multimedia elements.
- HTML+TIME is an implementation of SMIL that is included with Microsoft Internet Explorer v5.5 and above.
- SMIL shares many structures for timed page elements with SVG.
- SMIL presentations are constructed around timelines.
- Timelines can exist in series, in parallel, or on an exclusive basis.
- SMIL provides powerful structures for integrating media objects such as video and audio into web presentations.
- The SMIL animation elements enable timely control of any addressable attribute of any page element.
- Intermediate values in animations can be calculated linearly, or by some spline function.
- A range of transitions can be applied to the appearance or removal of an element on a page. Transitions can be applied in parallel to achieve more complex effects.

FURTHER INFORMATION

http://www.w3.org/AudioVideo/
The home of SMIL on the web – the WWW Consortium.

http://msdn.microsoft.com/library/default.asp?url=/workshop/author/behaviors/time.asp
An introduction to HTML+TIME.

http://www.w3.org/TR/NOTE-HTMLplusTIME
HTML+TIME reference from W3C.

http://homepages.cwi.nl/~media/SMIL/Tutorial/
Selection of tutorials implemented in SMIL.

http://www.helio.org/products/smil/tutorial/
Downloadable SMIL tutorial.

http://www.w3schools.com/smil/default.asp
Interactive examples from W3Schools.

http://hotwired.lycos.com/webmonkey/00/41/index4a.html
Introduction to SMIL with background, context and examples.

http://smw.internet.com/smil/tutor/
Collection of SMIL and HTML+TIME tutorials and examples.

http://www.helio.org/products/smil/tutorial/chapter1/index.html
A comprehensive SMIL tutorial.

http://www.htmlgoodies.com/htmltime.html
Background and introduction to HTML+TIME.

EXERCISES

1. Implement each of the code examples provided in the text. Try modifying various parameters and attributes in each example until you are comfortable with their operation.

2. Use HTML+TIME to produce a short slide-show presentation, where the individual slides are presented in a loop. Each slide should be constructed as a HTML DIV element, and should be displayed for 10 seconds in turn.

3. Modify the slideshow presentation constructed in Exercise 2 to build an interactive gallery. A series of thumbnail images should be presented as a menu, from which the user clicks on one to examine more closely. On clicking a thumbnail, the corresponding image is presented at full size, together with some text elements that describe its title, artist and any other relevant information.

4. Present a television news bulletin as a SMIL presentation. The bulletin should consist of a series of items, each described by an image, some audio voiceover and a title or series of captions. Use transitions as the bulletin moves from one item to the next.

5. Construct a web-based media retrieval and composition system. The system should provide an interface for the selection of media elements (images, video, audio, text etc.), and their placement into a timeline. The SMIL/HTML+TIME code to represent the timeline should then be automatically generated, so that the animation or presentation can be played independently of the composition system.

Index

visibility property 88
Visual Basic 95

W

W3C 6, 26–27
wallclock() 222
WAV 27
wave filter 85–86
while statement 102
width attribute 7, 14, 22, 26,
47–48, 133–134, 165–167,
196, 204–205, 245–246, 247
window object 113

window.clearInterval()
120–121
window.prompt() 98
window.setInterval()
120, 147
Windows XP 129

X

x attribute 133–134, 165,
170, 179–180, 196, 203
x1 attribute 174, 192
x2 attribute 174, 192
XHTML 2

xlink:href 186–187
XML (Extensible Markup
Language) 164
xray filter 84

Y

y attribute 133–134, 165,
170, 179–180, 196, 203
y1 attribute 174, 192
y2 attribute 174, 192

Z

z-index attribute 55